MAKING

DYING

JOYFUL

Stories of Companionship

Gail Bennett Owens

Hidden Lighthouse Publishers

http://fullservicepublishing.wordpress.com

Email: info@hiddenlighthouse.com

Page design and composition by Vicky Anderson

Cover design: Colin Owens and Jesse Owens

Making Dying Joyful
First Edition

ISBN 978-1491063101

Dedication

to the Concourse on High and my angels of
enthusiasm

Dear Aunt Anne!
Thanks for bringing
so much joy to life.
much love!

Sail

The names of the persons whose stories are told in this book have been changed out of respect for their families.

Contents

Foreword

When I was a medical intern, one of my duties was to pronounce the death of patients in the hospital. I knew nothing about the person who had died, and I don't recall ever meeting a family member. I had the sacred task of declaring the end of a life as if it were a clerical detail. Who was this being whose life was now over? What if we had met and cared about each other?

When I finished my internship, Michael Downing, the first Director of Hospice Victoria, invited me to train in Palliative Care and then to work with the Hospice along with my family practice. The training was a breath of fresh air in a world where many of us working in hospitals seemed to avoid patients when there was no longer hope for cure. Just when the patients and families most needed our support, we somehow pulled back.

The new movement to provide loving and compassionate care for the end of life grew in the next decades, and working in a hospice setting was a deeply rewarding part of my life.

Gail Owens shows us, through stories of men and women she has cared for, the gifts we receive by being with those near death. Unexpected laughter and moments of closeness are sometimes so intense we feel we have known this person for years. People show their lifelong strengths and their long held eccentricities, but often at the end, they shed their enmities and resolve old grievances in ways that give us inspiration to try to find that grace in ourselves. And sometimes they don't.

Taking on the role of a compassionate friend to someone calls on our deepest beliefs about the value of life and what may follow. Sometimes the insights we gain are uncomfortable and painful, often revealing our own shortcomings, our own lack of patience and forbearance. Sometimes we find something in ourselves that we didn't know was there. I am reminded of seeing great tenderness from nurses caring for drug addicts and the homeless - patients who had lived on the edges. I have to pause to wonder where the nurses found this selfless generosity of heart.

Gail's stories reveal the wholeness of each person she accompanies through loneliness, loss of memories, loss of capabilities and eventually loss of life itself.

I share her cherishing of funerals as a way to know and rejoice in the unique life that has ended.

Her work of Making Dying Joyful is a warm and loving gift to those who may have seen only the sorrow and emptiness of facing the death of a loved one.

Mary-Wynne Ashford

Introduction

"Getting old isn't easy you know," quipped one of my elderly clients. I think she was doing her own version of Bette Davis' famous line, "Old age ain't no place for sissies!"

No matter how it's expressed, it's a long haul into the sunset. That's for sure. At least, that's what I've been told. It seems as though I have been keeping company with the aged for a very long time. Some of my earliest memories involve going door-to-door after getting off of the school bus and finding a senior citizen home, ready to pour me a cup of tea.

The first year out of high school was indecisive for me, so my mother insisted that I volunteer. I chose a local care home. Perhaps I gravitated there because my own grandfather, who lived hundreds of miles away, had been diagnosed with Alzheimer's Disease a few years earlier.

I cherished my grandparents and, after my grandfather's eventual passing, I spent a lot of time with my grandmother. She invited me to Arizona where she wintered with other "snowbirds." The two of us would have meals with the other seniors. We would often venture off on our own and visit museums and parks together. One time, she admonished me after I thanked her for a fun outing. "It's alright to have fun dear, but what did you learn?"

Besides soaking in a lot of history and nature, I also learned the following:

- Listening to stories over and over makes us better storytellers.
- Developing patience is a useful skill.
- Laughing at ourselves feels good.
- Delegating tasks is smart.

I put all of this to good use, especially when I started volunteering for the Spiritual Care Department in a local hospital. There was a course offered to people who were willing to walk the spiritual path with patients. The criteria called for a listening ear, and an open and unbiased mind. After completing the course, it was a natural choice for me to begin visits on the geriatric ward.

It wasn't long before a social worker on the ward noticed that I seemed to have a knack with the elderly. "Have you ever thought of being a paid companion?" She asked. Shortly after that, I became swamped with referrals. It was a good "problem" to have.

Over the years, families have thanked me repeatedly for being good company for their parents. Although it felt nice to be appreciated, I didn't know why they showered me with so much gratitude until my own father got dementia. He got lost a few blocks from his home and wound up in the hospital. Thus began my own journey of navigation through the medical system. It involved consulting with doctors, consoling my mother, attempting to quell my father's agitation and informing family members of the situation. Ultimately, I had to make some hard choices that, in the end, involved selecting a care home for my dad.

I had always vowed that, when the time came, I would never put my parents in an institution. I felt that my husband and I could care for them in our own home. I felt that my experience as a companion to those who had memory problems would sustain me and I would deal well with whatever came my way. That was not the case. I soon learned that dealing with one's own parents is a whole different ball game.

It wasn't long before I developed a mild case of "care giver burnout." Luckily, it dawned on me that, I too, could hire a paid companion. Thankfully, our family friend agreed to visit Dad in his new care home a couple of times a week. Confident in her ability, I found that I could breathe again. That's when I finally understood the gratitude that had come my way from those families.

The ocean of thankfulness splashed over me and, along with it, there came new insights. Deposited like grains of sand, I found wisdom, detachment, humility and reliance on prayer. The tide of tranquility flows in and out, as needed and, through story telling, I can honor those who I have been with in their last months, days and minutes.

My absolute belief is that this life here on Earth is temporary; the soul of a person is eternal. It has given me a rather calm perspective on dying. Without a shadow of a doubt, I recognize that the hindrances and infirmities of the mind and body do not affect the soul. The testimony of this is evident in the lives of those people whom you will read about in this book. They have made a lasting impression on me. Their stories needed to be told, from my heart to yours.

The poet, Rumi, wrote that our death is our wedding day with eternity. "Your mouth closes here and immediately opens with a shout of joy there!" As we know, tears often accompany both births and weddings. My own sage advice is, "always have a box of tissues nearby!"

And when the earth shall claim your limbs,
then shall you truly dance.

Kahlil Gibran

Marie

When I met Marie she was in her early eighties. Her daughter had called me on the telephone and explained to me that her mother was living in a care home. Marie wanted to leave the premises, so I was asked to visit her a few times a week because she was running the staff ragged.

Marie's daughter went on to explain that she, too, needed a break from trying to keep her mother happy. Like most family members do, she was feeling guilty about the fact that her mother had been placed in a care home. Perhaps it wasn't that she felt guilt, rather, she just felt bad that she couldn't always be there for her.

Marie was suffering from a form of dementia. Living at home had become more and more stressful for her husband as well. Certainly placing her in such an institution was hard on him, but he was a devoted man who made the best of a bad situation and visited her most afternoons. It was the mornings that needed to be covered by someone else.

Initially, it was tricky for me to determine who all of the people in Marie's life were. She spoke about her sister a lot. I soon caught on that the "sister" of whom she spoke was actually her daughter and, when she referred to her "father," she actually meant her husband.

Marie

Then there were the other "sisters." Marie was raised as a Catholic and attended convent school, so she thought the care home was a Catholic boarding school and that all of the people who looked after her were nuns. They certainly didn't dress like nuns though.

There was to be no smoking in her room and, until her cigarettes were taken away from her and stored at the nursing station, it was a rule she liked to break. The "sisters" kept her closet locked so that she could not dress and redress. In order to go out with her, I had to ask for the key from the care aid so I could retrieve her coat from the closet. I also had to ask to get one of her cigarettes out of the stash they had locked away so she could smoke one when she left the building.

Sometimes she managed to get her coat first and would be waiting for me when I stepped off of the elevator. Although I wasn't late, she was usually quite worked up. "Where have you been?" she would ask angrily and, "Thank God you're here! Let's get outta here." There was no way she wanted to remain in the building. She wanted freedom. She wanted to get out in the fresh air and get some smoke into her lungs!

The two of us would walk to my car, arm in arm, and off we'd go. Usually, we would travel to O'Beans where Trevor, the owner, would greet us with a big smile and a wave. If Marie had already lit her cigarette, I'd grab the decaf, while she sat out on the patio. I positioned myself so that I would have a good view of her through the window. That way, if she made a move to get up, I could be out there in a flash.

Most days she would stay put and, as soon as I had paid Trevor, I would be out the door to join her. Real coffee pepped her up too much, and the combination of the nicotine and caffeine would make her heart race. Only once I made the mistake of ordering her caffeinated coffee. It was decaf from that point on!

Marie always attempted to pay me. Quite often, she had something jingling in her coin purse - a few quarters, or a dollar or two, which her daughter had supplied her with. Having some spending money made her feel normal. She'd open up her coin purse, inspect the contents and dump money out.

"Do I have enough for another one of those things?"

"What things?" I would ask, knowing full well that she meant a cigarette.

"You know, those sticks," she would say, sounding desperate.

The words may have escaped her, but the message was clear! Occasionally, I'd give in and buy her a cigarette from someone who was smoking nearby. Operating as her broker, I'd say, "My friend here would like to offer you a dollar for a cigarette." Fellow smokers are kindred spirits and I was always handed a cigarette with a knowing smile and, most of the time, there was no charge.

Marie enjoyed puffing on her cigarette much more than she did drinking her beverage. We would visit in her limited, but animated, way. She'd frequently mix up her words, but it wasn't too difficult to deduce what she was talking about. Our conversations usually went something like this...

"I went with that guy yesterday," she says.

"Who?"

"That guy," she replies, sounding irritated. "You know, my father."

"Oh, you mean Bert, your husband?"

"Yeah, him."

"So, go on."

"Well, we went for a drive and we went to that place."

Now I start guessing, "What place? The mall?"

"No. We went way out there to show him these." She motions to her eyeglasses.

"Oh, you went to the eye doctor?"

"Yeah, that's it," she sounds exasperated.

"So, go on." I smile.

"So this dame says that she can't do anything about these and I need new ones." Oh how I loved her language. Quite often, she inserted "dame" or "broad" into a sentence when she referred to someone with whom she was peeved.

Our time together went quickly and, before long, I would have her back at the care home. I always left her with a reassurance that her husband or daughter would be visiting after lunch and that I would see her again in a day or two.

Marie

True to my word, I would show up and she'd give me a repeat performance. As I stepped off of the elevator, she'd greet me impatiently, looking for me to rescue her from her captive existence. It was a carbon copy of the last time I was there.

Occasionally, we would see the traveling music therapist going from unit to unit. She would say with a kind smile, "Hi Marie. Would you like to join me? What song would you like to sing?" Marie would usually be hell bent for leather to get out, but sometimes she would agree to stop and sing, *It's a long way to Tipperary*, or some other wartime song.

Continuing on our way, we had to pass through the activity area. Sometimes there would be a bingo game or an exercise class in progress and, once a week, there was a church service. "Would you like to stay for mass, Marie?" the volunteer would ask. "No, thank you," Marie would reply, "I'm going out with my friend."

Once or twice, we sat through a very short Easter or Thanksgiving service, at her husband's insistence. Her family was always happy when I informed them that we had almost managed to stay to the end of the sermon.

Many days there would be carpet bowling or a group sing-a-long with some campy entertainer. "Hey, Marie!" they'd yell when she breezed past, "Care to join us today?" "No thanks," she would usually reply. She was restless and getting out would always do her good.

This routine continued for a couple of years. I would visit Marie on Monday, Wednesday and Friday, between 10:00 and

17

11:30 a.m. Sometimes we'd chat in her room a bit, spending time looking at the photographs that hung on her wall. "That's my mother", she'd say, pointing to a picture of herself. She thought that she was still a young girl and, because the older lady in the picture looked so familiar, she thought it must be her mother.

One day I walked into her room and the first thing she said to me was, "I have to get something for my face."

"Like what?" I queried.

"Well, you know, something for this."

She led me to the mirror and showed me that her face was all wrinkled and sagging. I smiled and assured her that we would get her some cream. The next day, I brought Marie some little sample packages of Avon hydrating and anti-wrinkle face cream. She delighted in rubbing it gently all over her aging face.

The days and weeks went by and, as was to be expected, Marie's health deteriorated. Her daughter told me that her mother had been diagnosed with an aortic aneurysm and that the doctor advised against an operation, so it really was kind of a ticking time bomb in her abdomen.

Her back became incredibly painful, as well. I put liniment on it for her and, a couple of times, her family gave me permission to take her to my chiropractor. Of course, my chiropractor knew that she had dementia and other health issues, so he treated her very professionally, gently adjusting her frail body.

One November day, I received a call from Marie's daughter. She told me that her mother had developed pneumonia and was not expected to live through the day. I rushed to her bedside, "Marie," I said, "It's me, Gail." She nodded and I said, "We've had some good times, you and I."

She appeared to mumble something. I held her hand and said, "You know you're loved." She said, "Uh huh," and nodded in agreement. Then I leaned over her, moved in close to her ear and whispered, "I love you very much." Between her labored breathing and gasps, I heard her say, "I love you too darling." After that, I left her room so that she could be alone with her family. A few hours later, Marie's daughter telephoned to say that her mother had left this world.

Marie's funeral was held at the Catholic cathedral. It was large and grand, and full of ritual. It was traditional of Catholic send-offs and, as is customary, there is a liturgy that focuses on the spiritual message of the promise of life after death. The priest offered prayers for eternal rest and perpetual light to shine upon Marie. That being said, I did think of her a lot. I felt a closeness and a connection, especially when the soloist sang *Ave Maria*. Her voice, clear and rich, echoed off of the cathedral walls and ceiling.

The beautiful aria about Mary, the mother of Christ, translates literally as "Hail Mary." The words, "*listen to a maiden's prayer, safe may we sleep beneath thy care,*" resonated deeply with me. Tears fell from my face as I listened to the Latin, "*Ora pro nobis, et in hora mortis nostrae.*" Pray for us sinners now and at the hour of death.

Marie

Marie's final years had been spent in a mental haze. But, at last, her soul had found tranquility. *Pax Domini sit semper vobiscum...*

The words went up, up...

May the peace of the Lord be always with you.

Tip:

Bring an old photo album and go down memory lane together.

Maggie

Maggie and I first met when she was a patient in a local hospital. She had come from a rather exclusive, senior's assisted living residence. The circumstances surrounding her admission were such that her 92 year old husband, Bob, was run ragged while he was trying to take care of her, so she was admitted to hospital and was waiting to be transferred to a care facility that could better meet her needs.

Maggie had an extreme curvature of the spine. She also had osteoporosis, which confined her to a wheelchair. Although robust for his age, her husband no longer had the strength to lift her wheelchair in and out of the trunk of their car. He still drove and mentally he was as fit as a fiddle.

On the other hand, Maggie was deteriorating both mentally and physically, and had recently suffered a serious fall. The place in which they were living could no longer house her. She simply required too much care - the kind that is more consistent with an extended care facility, so Bob and Maggie were being separated. This is often the case with aging seniors whose needs become complex and diverse.

The transition from living as man and wife for more than 60 years was going to be a tough one for this couple, so the social worker at the hospital asked me if I could be Maggie's companion in order to aid with the adjustment to her new home.

Maggie

Shortly thereafter, I started visiting Maggie at a care facility where a roommate had taken the place of her husband. Immediately, the separation was stressful for her. She and her husband had never raised children. As well, she had been an only child and was accustomed to being doted on.

At her new accommodation she sat at a table in the dining hall with three other women. She and another lady were extremely hard of hearing, so attempting to keep some conversation flowing, without angering anyone, made for an interesting situation. Offence was easily taken, not by myself, but by Maggie and her tablemates. They glared at one another as they consumed their food, so I became the appetite coach and mediator...

"Are you having a nice day?" asked Annie.

Maggie replied, "Eh?" and gave me a bewildered look.

"Annie is asking you if you're having a nice day."

"Who?" she said, looking really puzzled.

"Annie, here beside you."

"What?"

"She wants to know if you're having a nice day."

"I guess it's alright."

By this time, Annie has taken offence to our conversation because she can't hear us. I smile and translate, "Maggie says her day is going fine." Then I add, "She misses her husband." I decide that it is a good idea to offer an explanation as to why Maggie is looking so sour.

Maggie

Maggie wasn't always sour though. She would join in activities if either I or the activity coordinator coaxed her. She would smile sweetly whenever she was given extra attention and care. She enjoyed getting weekly manicures and having her hair washed and styled.

Most of the time, when I wasn't present, or when she wasn't eating a meal or joining in some exercise circle, she would position her wheelchair in the hall so that she could watch for her husband's arrival for his daily visit.

One of the highlights of that time was the celebration of Maggie's ninetieth birthday. Her nieces and nephews, and their spouses and children were all invited. On the afternoon of her big day, we had a nice little tea party with fine bone china. Applications were made in plenty of time to ensure that letters from Canadian dignitaries, such as the Prime Minister and Governor General, were on hand. The Governor General sent a nice letter of congratulations on behalf of Her Majesty, Queen Elizabeth. An official letter from Her Majesty is not issued until a person celebrates their one-hundredth birthday. I suspect the reason behind that is simply because there would be far too many requests.

After that milestone day, I would remind Maggie that she was 90 years old. She had a hard time fathoming that and she told me that some things just seemed to be pure nonsense! Although she liked some attention, she really didn't like a whole lot of fuss, especially when she was ill or in a bad mood. However, without that extra attention, she would have been very confused and sad.

Maggie liked to recall the past and I gave her a listening ear. During those times, she would often mention her mother who was widowed when Maggie was a little girl. She informed me that, years later, her mother came to live with her and Bob. A photograph of her mother was prominently displayed close to her bedside. It was obvious that they had enjoyed a close bond.

No matter where Maggie was transferred to live, the photograph was always displayed near her. It was a testament to her devotion. Maggie was moved quite a bit, so the photo helped with the transition.

It seemed cruel to me to move someone so elderly from one place to another. It happens all the time though - couples getting separated due to healthcare cuts. Maggie and a dozen other patients were moved to a temporary building. It was a building that had been slated for closure at one time, but was then reopened. She was given a temporary room there for a couple of months.

While she was living there, a gentleman with an advanced case of Alzheimer's disease pursued her. He just wanted to hold her hand, but she found that distressing. The poor man was really quite harmless and I found him to be quite likeable. However, Maggie was frightened of his behavior and had no tolerance for him. Thankfully she was moved from that building to another facility, which was a bit better, but she had another roommate yet again.

Maggie

These series of moves really took their toll on her and always upset her stomach. The stress created breathing difficulties and more memory problems as well. We were lucky that she survived. Many seniors do not survive and the move literally kills them.

No matter where Maggie moved, though, her devoted Bobby, as she adoringly called him, would visit faithfully every day at 2:00 p.m. The two of them would have tea together and chat. Then, when there was nothing more to say, he would just sit with her and work on a crossword puzzle. Before dinner he would head back to the retirement home where he lived.

Bob had maintained his membership with a local golf club and was managing to play nine holes of golf once a week. He was quite a remarkable man and, for the first year or so of their separation, he was still driving his car to visit her. Even after his own health started to fail and he gave up his driver's license, he would walk three city blocks from his residence to hers!

My morning visits were a great help to her husband and he expressed his gratitude. He said they were a reassurance for him that Maggie would not be lonely. Our arrangement was that I would stay with her through lunch, and then he would come and see her after her nap.

Maggie always watched for him. If he had to stay home due to a bout of ill health, she would be extremely disappointed. If he was going to be absent for an extended amount of time, I arranged my visits so they would last longer. Quite often, their niece would stop by and join her aunt for a cup of afternoon tea.

Even with all of this attention, it was hard for Maggie to settle in at her final stop, which was the Dunedin Seniors Care Home. It wasn't because of poor treatment or anything like that. The staff was marvelous. They were very loving and gentle with her. It's just that Maggie was set in her ways, and the upheaval and separation were both hard on her. For the first few months after her transfer, she would ask me, "Where am I?" to which I would reply, "You're at Dunedin."

She would say, "Where?"

I would repeat, "Dunedin. It's a care home."

"Well, where is it?"

"It's on Hill Avenue."

Again she would ask in a very irritated way, "WHAT IS DUNNEDIN?" and I would say patiently and softly, "Well, it's a care home and Bob lives nearby. He will be coming to see you as usual."

That answer would never satisfy her though and, every time I visited, I'd get the same series of questions. My answers always made her angry and her response was to grip her chair, bare her teeth and hiss, "Dunedin. Dunedin. It's always Dunedin!"

Since I could never please her with my answers, I began to get very evasive and, when she would ask, "Where am I?" I would dodge her question by saying things like, "You're in a care home," or, "It's like a hospital," or, "You're in Canada." I thought that

Maggie

telling her the name of the country might appease her. Maybe she thought Dunedin Care Home was actually Dunedin, Scotland! It never worked, though, at least not until one day when I had a revelation. I decided that I should tell her how I felt about her reaction. So, when she asked, "Where am I?" I replied, "Maggie, I'm not going to tell you because you always get angry with my answer."

"I do?" she asked. She was visibly surprised.

"Yes, you do. Your face gets angry looking and you get very upset when I tell you."

"I do?"

"Yes you do, and I don't know how to phrase it so I don't upset you."

"I'm sorry."

"If I tell you today the name of this place, do you promise not to get angry?"

"Yes. I promise."

"You're at Dunedin Care Home."

Maggie gripped the handles of her wheelchair very tight, and she sat very erect and trembled, but she maintained her composure. "Oh," she said quietly and she never asked me again!

Thankfully we continued to get along very well and, when I was with her, she was my number one priority. Besides being her companion, it was my job to take inventory of her clothes and to ensure that she had everything she needed in order to stay well dressed and happy. Often the care aids would either let Bob's

29

niece know or they would tell me what she needed. We would make the purchases on Maggie's behalf and Bob would write us a cheque. A note of genuine appreciation always accompanied his reimbursement.

Bob took care of his wife's sweet tooth and made sure there was always a box of 'deluxe cream' chocolates in her room! I was happy that Maggie always shared her wealth with me!

Her husband brought mail to her as well. She liked me to read her cards aloud. One Christmas card she displayed and was particularly proud of was from the Prime Minister of Canada. She made it known that she and Bob had been staunch and generous supporters. It made her very happy when I commented on it. As she looked at his photo on the front of the card, she floored me with her statement, "I like this prime minister." Then she added, "He's very sexy!" I found that especially funny coming from a reserved 92 year old and I shrieked with laughter.

Maggie was raised to be prim and proper. She often reminded me that her mother would "never approve of such things."

Unfortunately, moments of humor became few and far between, and Maggie's last few months on this earth were not easy. She was extremely frail. At one point, she broke her wrist while she was banging it on her bedside rail. As a result, she was put on a regime of painkillers and a mild sedative.

Due to complications and continuing ill health, Maggie steadily went downhill. Despite this, she always managed to give me a faint smile whenever I visited. She would murmur with appreciation when I gave her spoonfuls of yogurt, or when I would break off bits of chocolate and feed them to her encouragingly. When chewing became difficult for her, I brought her nourishing drinks so she could take a few sips.

Eventually, though, it became obvious that her old frail body couldn't take much more and she was nearing the end of her life. One of her favorite nurses informed me that my dear client did not have much time left. I reassured her that I would stay by Maggie's bedside so she wouldn't feel alone. This was a comfort for Maggie's husband who felt a sense of despair. He was now 95 years of age and they had been married nearly 70 years! I told him not to worry, that Maggie was as pain free as modern medicine allowed her to be and that I would be with her right up to the end.

That end came on a long weekend in May. I was with her at the very moment that her soul departed. It was a peaceful transition. Her blue eyes had become lighter, very much like the sky. They looked up toward Heaven as she took her final breath. The nurses and I hugged each other and cried. It was a privilege to spend those precious final hours with her.

Leaving the building, I remembered how Maggie had sat waiting for a familiar face each day, how she was genuinely pleased to see my face and how appreciative she had been. As I walked out into the bright sunlight, I looked up at the sky and felt the warmth on my face. I took a deep breath. The confusion for Maggie had ended and her pain was gone.

Maggie

As I stepped into my car, the lyrics of an old song popped into my mind and, before I knew it, I was singing, *"Blue skies smiling on me, nothing but blue skies do I see. Blue birds singing a song, nothing but blue skies from now on."*

Tip:

See if there's a project you can do with your senior such as helping with decorations, setting the table, folding laundry, etc.

Bob

A year or so after Maggie's passing, I received a call from her husband's niece asking me if I could now be his companion. She provided me with a wonderful account of how her Uncle Bob had grieved after his wife's passing but had continued with his routine, which included a daily walk around the block. She went on to say that he had suffered a couple of falls and requested that I accompany him so that he would have a hand to steady him if he should need it.

There had also been a promise made to his doctor that he would not go out on his own. Being a very independent man, Bob was used to managing very well, but agreed that his niece could call me and ask for my services.

Because of our previous connection with his wife, Maggie, we hit it off right away. We reminisced a little each day, while we went for our walks. Mainly, though, we exchanged pleasantries and made small talk. He could get quite frustrated by his health challenges. He would say, "I used to walk three blocks, without being tired." I would remind him that, at the age of 98 years, it was only natural that he would be slowing down a bit.

While Maggie was alive, he demonstrated that he was a man of commitment; he was a man of his word. He had survived the Second World War, had led troops and had been hit by shrapnel. He was frustrated that he could no longer manage with the relatively simple things in life.

Bob had golfed at a prestigious golf club and held a membership there until he was 94 years old. He had driven his newer model Honda until he was that age as well. Now he had to be "babysat" by many people. It was quite unsettling for him. Whenever we were together I did my best to let him make all the decisions.

Every morning, he dressed himself in really fine clothes. He never wore sweat pants, which was the favorite suggestion of nurse's aides who liked to keep things simple. His choice was always good quality dress pants and a nice dress shirt that he covered with a wool sweater. His jet-black hair showed only a hint of grey around the ears. It was always neatly combed. His shoes had cost him $500 dollars. They were custom made because he had been having foot problems. Five hundred dollars! Wow! I thought they looked like bedroom slippers with Velcro. I didn't say that aloud, thankfully!

We'd walk over to the local shopping mall at least once a week to pick up some things from his shopping list. He liked to buy items from the pharmacy to keep his teeth in fastidious condition. His regime consisted of brushing after every meal and before bed. He also used a special toothpick and rinsed at least once a day with mouthwash.

When we weren't out walking or running errands, we would sit in his room or in the main foyer of the residence doing something he really enjoyed - following the stock market. He'd open the business section of the newspaper and I would read him the figures because his eyesight wasn't the best. "Gold - up. Price of a barrel of oil - up. Your bank stock - down, but still pretty healthy." Of course that would make him very happy.

During our walks we would stop and smell the fragrance of the roses, identify species of flowers, or make chit chat with local homeowners who were out in their gardens. He told me of his past, which included fibbing about his age in order to get into the army.

Bob was born and raised on the west coast of Canada. He came from a large family and, to him, it was incredulous that he had outlived all of his brothers and sisters. At the end of our walks, we would go to the dining room together for refreshments. He would fill me in on some other historic facts over his cup of coffee and my cup of tea. I took pleasure in seeing his eyes light up when I put a tart or a cookie on his plate. I loved watching him eat every bite. Always a gentleman, Bob never missed a day without complimenting the waitress and the cook for the good food they provided.

With the good weather drawing to a close and another year on the calendar coming to an end, Bob grew more and more tired. Unfortunately, one morning before I arrived, he fell and broke his wrist. This accident was the beginning of real despair because he could no longer push his walker with the cast he had on. He ended up in a wheelchair, relying on others to push him where he wanted to go.

Bob

He lost interest in checking the stocks, in reading the newspaper and in watching television. Instead, he became content to just lie on his bed. If I suggested that we go for a walk, he became fearful of being too cold. However, with some encouragement, I could get him to get up and go for a little "push" around the block. I would dress him warmly in his cashmere sweater, and put a cap on his head and a scarf around his neck. Then out we would go.

He did remain interested in what I was up to, and what his nieces and their families were up to. There was nothing wrong with Bob's mind, only with his body. It was breaking down bit by bit.

I felt sorry for him when he wondered aloud, "Why am I still alive?" He had enjoyed his life but was ready to move on. That time came quickly and rather suddenly.

One morning, the staff at his retirement home noticed that he was extremely tired and that his speech was slurred. The nurse on duty called an ambulance for him and he was rushed to a local hospital. I visited him as soon as I heard the news. He couldn't speak, but he smiled at me and his eyes lit up, expressing appreciation.

I telephoned his niece to tell her about my visit and she told me about her uncle's living will. He had given his lawyer explicit instructions that, should the time come when he was unable to care for himself, he would "rather die" than have others look after him. Under no circumstances should heroic efforts be made to keep him alive artificially or to feed him through a tube.

Bob

Two days later, I went back to visit Bob at the hospital and discovered that he had passed away only minutes before I arrived. The nurse met me at the door and said that his nieces and their families had just left the premises. She went on to tell me that, just prior to his death, he appeared to be very aware and had been following them with his eyes. She added that, when they went to get a drink from the cafeteria, he had taken the opportunity to sigh his last breath. "It was as though he wanted it that way," she said. I agreed with her wholeheartedly. "Yes, he never wanted to be an inconvenience to anyone."

The young nurse indicated that, in the span of her short career, it was the first time she had seen a patient pass on so peacefully. "There were no death rattles and no labored breaths. Just a quick final breath, eyes shut and then, nothing." I thanked her for her kindness. That's what Bob would have done. She gushed that it was her privilege and that she was in awe of him. "Nearly a hundred years old and dark hair, with only a tiny bit of grey, and all his own teeth. Truly amazing!" "He *was* amazing," I replied. Then I asked her if I could have a couple of minutes with him before she took his body away. She said, "Of course," and then let me into his room.

It was brightly lit. He lay on the bed in the sunlight that was beaming in through the window. I stood silently wondering what to do, whether I should pray or just stand there in contemplation. I did a bit of both.

Bob

I thought about how this man had lived his life. He had been a perfect gentleman and a doting husband to dear Maggie. He was a man who had served his country during times of war, receiving medals for his valor. I whispered, "Good-bye old soldier. You did well." It just felt like the right thing to say. In my head, rang out the words that I had heard at veteran's memorials...

At the going down of the sun and in the morning, we will remember them.

Lord God of Hosts
Be with us yet,
Lest we forget,
Lest we forget.

Tip:

Bring a new silk flower arrangement in to make the room cheery. There's no need to worry about watering the plant. It will only need to be dusted once in a while.

Angela

One of the care homes offered my business card to a lady by the name of Lynn and I received a call a short time later. It was explained to me that, as the appointed Power of Attorney, she made all of the business and living decisions for an elderly woman named Angela. She asked me to provide some intellectual stimulation for Angela, via good conversation and outings.

Angela was extremely bright. She was a retired, psychiatrist. Unfortunately, as a result of some form of surgery, her brain had been deprived of oxygen. She had suffered some transient ischemic attacks and was having memory issues, as well.

As a gifted artist, sculptor and patron of the arts, and the holder of a Ph.D, Angela needed something more to do than just sitting around the common area of the nursing station. She needed something more than carpet bowling and bingo to keep her mind occupied and to stave off depression. It was ironic that someone who had helped others combat mental illness during her lifetime was now the one who was in need. She was extremely frustrated in her care home environment.

Our visits together always began with her saying "So, how are you?" followed by, "How are the kiddies?" and, "What have you been up to?" If I tried to turn the conversation around and inquire as to her wellbeing, she would often flip it back my way as if she was analyzing me by asking, "How are you feeling?" or, "How does that make you feel?"

When I first started companioning Angela, she actually had a boyfriend of sorts - a gentleman by the name of Vern who lived across the hall. He seemed like an unlikely suitor - she, the scholarly and uprooted Jewish Montrealer and he, a bit of a cowboy and her polar opposite. Nonetheless, he was smitten with her and would sit next to her, patting her hand and professing his undying love for her.

Initially, Angela was quite charmed by Vern's affections. However, she had been a single lady for most of her life, other than a brief marriage and divorce. This newfound attention seemed to make her a bit claustrophobic.

Whenever she saw me, she'd jump right up, eager to go for a drive. We'd head to the waterfront, and then get out of the car to sit on a bench and chat, while we took in the scenery. She enjoyed watching people walk their dogs, or play with their children. Sometimes we'd just sit in my vehicle with the radio tuned to a classical music station. It was fun to see her hands wave in the air as she "conducted" an imaginary orchestra, while we watched hang-gliders and floatplanes fly overhead. They seemed to move in time to the music! Her mood could be quite changeable, though, and she expressed frustration and sometimes even anger about her dementia. That would be my cue to start driving again and she would soon forget her problems as I redirected her attention.

"Let's go get a treat, Angela."

Angela

It became a priority to get her warmed and get some nutritious food into her. Her circulation was very poor and her hands often looked and felt cold. Her place of residence generally served processed foods, like canned soup and canned fruit, so it was a pleasure to take her out for "real" soup, fresh fruit salad and a cup of decent coffee. We had a couple of favorite haunts, one of which was a place called Lloyd's Diner. During good weather, we'd sit outside on the patio and bask in the sunshine.

Another time or two we went to a great café near the waterfront and, although the noise level could be quite high during lunch hour, we had fun watching people. It seemed like most of the clientele were professional types who were engaged in animated business dealings.

Due to her mental fog, Angela was incapable of changing the channel on her television or of inserting a CD into the proper place. She couldn't remember how to tune the radio dial. Many times, when I left her in her room at the end of our visit, I'd leave her with something interesting to watch or listen to. I took care to ensure that the volume wasn't set too high because the slightest irritation could set her off on a tirade with the staff.

She wasn't always cantankerous, however. Most of the time, I was able to see her sweet side. During many of our visits, her face displayed a sweet and contented smile as I read poetry to her, or an interesting article from the Globe and Mail. She seemed keen to hear it. If she were having trouble processing a thought, sometimes she would ask me to repeat. Although her monthly psychiatry journals were sent to her, they remained primarily unread. I suspect that either she didn't want to be reminded of her former profession, or perhaps she was unable to comprehend the complex writing.

Often I would see her with a paperback book she was trying to read, although she would seldom, if ever, actually get through it cover-to-cover. She'd generally forget her place, and then read and re-read the lines. Many times, she'd nod off and have an extended afternoon nap with the book lying on her chest.

If she awoke in a good mood, we'd have some interesting conversation. After she quizzed me for a while, I'd prod her to remember her childhood. She told me about her brother, and about her parents and grandparents. Growing up as a Jew in wartime Hungary, she'd experienced the hatred of the Nazis. She had been moved from pillar to post and had lived in a concentration camp. It was something that she wouldn't dwell on. She would quickly change the subject. She chose to reminisce about fun things, instead, such as swimming in the lake near the home of her grandparents. She loved to swim and considered herself to be a good swimmer.

One hot summer day, I took her to a local lake, even though I was a bit apprehensive, given her dementia, declining health and unsteadiness. Assisting her in the ladies change room was particularly challenging because she really resented me helping her out of her clothes and into her swimsuit. I insisted, though, because the floors were concrete and slippery, and a fall could have had dire consequences. I battled her uncooperativeness and told her that, if she would let me help her, we could have a nice swim in the lake.

Eventually, we made it down to the beach. Once we were standing upon the sand, Angela was eager to get into the water and experience freedom - the kind that weightlessness brings. She waded in happily and, before long, she was performing the motions of an experienced, competent swimmer. I'll never forget the joy on her face, as she stood in the water with the warm sun beating down.

One day, after summer had turned into fall, Angela fell in her bathroom at the care home and broke her hip. After that, her mobility was never the same, but I still did my best to turn dull into bright and stubborn into agreeable. She could be demanding, prone to outbursts of anger and hard for the staff to manage. I, however, could generally soothe the savage beast of a downtrodden and unhappy Angela. If I noticed that she was agitated, I could usually find the right words with which to reason with her. She almost always turned on the charm while in my presence.

If she was having a bad day, she would refuse the efforts of the care aids to get her out of bed. I'd come in and find her with the bedding pulled right up to her chin. Immediately I'd set to work in an effort to dispel the greyness she was feeling. I'd tear open the curtains to let the natural light in, sometimes even dancing at the end of her bed to see if I could stop her from glowering. I did my utmost to bring a ray of sunshine into her room - if not literally, then figuratively.

"How 'bout a hand massage, Angela?" I'd ask.

"Baaaa," was her reply.

"C'mon, let me pamper you."

"I don't want to be pampered. I want to sleep."

To this I would open the lid of the Zen hand cream and let her sniff the fragrance. "See. Wouldn't that smell good on you? It's a very relaxing scent, isn't it?" It wouldn't take any more persuading and, soon, I was massaging it into her hands.

Many elderly people stop taking care of themselves in a personal way. But Angela liked to look good. She liked to put on lipstick and she always combed her hair. She'd often forget to brush her teeth though, and had to be prompted to do so. As most people with dementia or Alzheimer's do, she often forgot what she had eaten for lunch, let alone when she last had a haircut. That's why, every couple of months, I'd seek out the hairdressing staff at the little salon on the first floor of the care home and, together, we'd try to coax our friend, Angela, in for a trim. She had lovely hair and, when it was tidied up, it really looked decent.

Another place I had to accompany her was to the mobile dentist. The folks in the care home were fortunate enough to have a dentist and a dental assistant come to visit. They'd set up shop for one day, every three months, in a meeting room on the first floor. The staff couldn't talk Angela into going for a check-up. I, on the other hand, could always persuade her.

Angela

We'd go down the elevator together and, just when the doors would open, I'd explain that we had arrived for her dental appointment. "I'll stay with you Angela, I promise," and in through the door we would go. It was a small victory. I had succeeded in curbing her agitation and the hygienist appreciated it.

Once she was seated in the chair, Angela became quite pleasant for the most part. She would chat and joke with the dentist. I think she still recognized that he was a professional, like herself, and thought of him as a peer in the medical profession. She never forgot her life's work as a psychiatrist. It's the short-term stuff, the recent endeavors, which don't stick around, and Angela's memory for conversation and events was about five minutes long, at the very most.

In spite of all of the frustration she voiced and all of the complaining she did, I really enjoyed being with Angela. I loved looking at her sculptures and the art she had created in bygone years. I tried to encourage her creative side - to get in touch with her inner artist. Once or twice I brought in a sketchbook and some colored pencils. She drew a little, but expressed embarrassment. She thought that it was childlike to create on paper. "I can't concentrate anymore!" and "I don't have the skill," she said. Always gracious, though, she thanked me for being with her.

After Vern, her gentleman friend, passed away, I tried taking her on a "double date." I arranged for another paid companion at the care home and her male client to join us for a drive and a picnic in the park. Angela and the man I had invited were both of the cultured type and they both shared a good sense of humor, so it went rather well. Unfortunately, after that day, whenever the two of them would meet in the halls of the care home, it was as if they were being introduced for the very first time. No lasting friendship was made, but at least I tried.

On one occasion, I brought Angela to a multi-faith celebration. She was very accepting of other people and of other religions, so I thought she would get something out of the uplifting program and from being around vibrant folks who were engaging in some "real" conversation. It was a nice change for her from her care home environment where the element of true conversation is often lacking. She looked "normal" and no one really caught on that she had dementia. She was intellectually stimulated and really felt like she belonged.

From time to time, we engaged in limited debates about science and religion, and about whether or not there really is a God. I read to her from the writings of many faiths and she was candid about her doubts. She felt that, with her scientific background, the two concepts did not go hand-in-hand. She thought that world peace sounded nice, but also rather utopic and not very practical. That was until I brought her a book of poetic scripture that was written in her native Hungarian. "Here, read this," I said, as I handed it over to her. I don't read Hungarian, but I owned the same book in English, so I knew the gist of what it said. After she read it, she paused for a moment. Then she said, "These words are very potent and touching." The elevated nature of the writing, which was relayed in her mother tongue, had seemed to really touch her heart and, perhaps, even her soul.

As the years went by, Angela grew more and more unhappy with her situation, and I found myself being able to do less and less with her as far as going on outings. One day, after we completed a trip to see an exhibit at the art gallery, she vomited in my car. I couldn't take her after that because she felt nauseous much of the time. It was a side effect of one of her medications. Even though we didn't go out much anymore, we had some good dialogue. In moments of calmness, she said things that were really profound. She looked at me once and said, "You know, it's one thing to be losing your mind and not know it. But to lose your mind and know it is a very sad thing."

During another visit, I had pen and paper in hand when she spoke this gem… "Being alone isn't a bad thing, but not knowing what to do with your aloneness IS a bad thing." Later on, she said to me, "I didn't fill my life with the right things." I tried to assure her that she had. I reminded her of her gift for art. I pointed to her clay sculptures and to her framed drawings, which were hanging on the wall. She nodded with a smile.

It was shortly after that when a change took place in her. Her demeanor became more complacent and her attitude was more accepting of her situation. She said that she was at peace and could leave this world at any time.

The day when Angela passed away I was not with her but, fortunately, her friend Lynn was. I was in attendance at her funeral, though, which was held at the Jewish Cemetery on a hot summer day. Those who came from the local synagogue walked happily behind the rabbi, chanting many things in Hebrew. Some of it was repeated in English and one particular sentence resonated with me. "May she go to her resting place in peace." I knew that Angela had indeed done that. I recalled that summer day, a year or two earlier, when we swam together in the lake. It felt good to imagine that she was now swimming once again, in an *Ocean of Light*. *

Tip:

Find a corner, a nook, a sunroom or an atrium in which you can read poetry or something spiritual together. If it's appropriate, recite a prayer.

Elise

One day, my contact information was forwarded to the trust company that looked after the matters of an elderly woman, named Elise. The trustee had called me to ask if I could visit Elise who had no known family in the area. The care home thought she could do with some stimulation.

When I first met Elise, I was astonished by her physical size. Even though she was sitting in a wheelchair, I could see that she was a tall, erect woman with large hands.

She didn't speak much and she didn't make a lot of sense when she did talk. She was a joy to listen to, though. When she spoke, she had a hint of a British accent and often used a punishing tone. She had beautiful eyes and a lovely smile. I enjoyed making her laugh and making those eyes light up. She had short straight hair and her complexion was a rosy, peach color.

Her closets were bursting with fine clothes. She owned handsome coats and cashmere sweaters that bore tags from Harrods in London. Her drawers contained silk scarves and, in her wallet, there was a membership card for the Natural Historical Society. To me, they were all indications of an intelligent and well-to-do existence.

Initially, she and I would sit by the faux fireplace and flip through a book or magazine together. I would comment on pictures and articles, and she would always respond accordingly and on cue. For exercise, I would toss a balloon or a soft ball for her to catch. Her coordination was still very good and she had good reflexes.

A couple of times, as I was trying to give her a drink, she scared the life out of me when she took a swat! Once, her hands darted at me so fast that I screamed and spilled a chocolate nourishment supplement all over myself, her bed and the floor as well! At that moment, her flash of anger turned to laughter. It must have been a very funny sight for her!

Those types of episodes were all in a day's work for me. Sometimes I went beyond the call of duty. Elise couldn't tell me about herself so I went out of my way in an attempt to gain some information about her from other sources. Surely, I surmised, there must be a family member somewhere in the world that would like to know that their aunt, or even their mother, was still alive.

Elise was into her nineties and there were a couple of photos showing her with both a man and a lady. However, there was nothing written on the backs of them to indicate who the people were. She also had a portrait studio photo of an older girl and a couple of younger girls. I wondered if, perhaps, they were her grandchildren. Had she had a falling out with her daughter? No letters came for her and no cards. Had she disappeared from everyone's radar?

The trustee gave me very little information. Actually, she couldn't say very much because Elise's file was new to her. She really didn't know much about Elise, other than that she had money.

It was amusing to take Elise out for short walks in the garden. Her face expressed delight and, on our way back into the building, she'd look at people and chuckle. Enroute back to her room we'd pass the care home's gift shop. One day, she surprised me when she saw a poster in the window that read, "Up to 50% off." She commented, "That's half off!" Besides reflexes, apparently math skills are one of the last things to go when you're losing your mind.

Whenever I would place literature in front of her, she would read poetry and verse aloud to me. She knew how the stanzas should be read and the cadence/speed of how they should be delivered. One day, I placed a Reader's Digest article in front of her, which was about NHL hockey player, Mario Lemieux. While she was scanning a paragraph in the article, she placed her finger on a date. Then she started repeating, "March 2nd." That was the date Mario finished his final radiation treatment for Hodgkin's disease, and then went on to score a goal on ice that very same evening! I couldn't figure out why Elise kept pointing at the date. "March 2nd," she said, over and over. Then it suddenly dawned on me that March 2nd was her birthday! I had seen it written in her records. Elise had a birth date of March 2, 1911. I thought it was amazing that she had picked up on that date. It was important to her, but she couldn't vocalize why.

Elise

Every year on her special day, I would bring her a small cake or cupcake with a candle atop. We'd have a little party with some of the other residents and staff. It made her smile from ear to ear. I'd assist her as she opened a small gift from all of us. One time I introduced her to my son and daughter, and then jokingly added, "Aren't they good looking?" To that, she replied, "To YOU maybe!" For years, my family laughed when we recalled her reaction!

As time went by, I began a more active search for her relatives and started to pry information from nurses. I received a lot of information from a substituting social worker. She had Elise's file and had jotted down the names of a couple of her nephews who were mentioned in her will as her next of kin. However, it soon became apparent that the surnames were incorrect and the names that I was given led to a dead end.

I puzzled over a photograph of her standing in front of a kind of seaside cottage. On the back, it read, "Clacton on Sea." Somehow, I managed to track down someone in the municipal hall at Clacton, in England, who kindly assisted me with the family search of the maiden name. It was then that I got a break and contacted a nephew of Elise's who lived in Ontario. He was thrilled that I had gone the extra mile to locate him. He told me that he suspected that his aunt was still alive. However, he had not been able to track her down because of privacy regulations and due to the fact that she had moved from her apartment years earlier.

Elise

At the request of the trustee, I went through Elise's belongings and itemized her things so that, when she passed away, they would know what she had in her possession. She had some marvelous jewelry, mainly costume, but of excellent quality - some rhinestones and a couple of nice sterling silver and pearl necklaces, and some broaches.

What fascinated me, though, were her leather-bound diaries. Elise had penned them upon her arrival in Canada from her native England, in the 1920's or 30's. Her handwriting was a bit difficult to read, not because it was sloppy, but because it was so flowery. Through her diaries, I learned that she and her husband, George, had never had any children.

Her storage locker also contained lots of books, mainly hard covers. It seemed that she liked to purchase the latest best sellers so, based on the information I had obtained and some of the items I was allowed to transport back to the care home, I managed to keep her reading and talking, and dressed in some of her nicest clothes and accessories.

After making contact with her nephews in Canada and in the U.K, she began to receive cards, letters, flowers and photos from them. Her sister had just recently passed away in England. I found it sad that I was just a bit too late with my research to help Elise reconnect with her sister on this plane of existence.

Nevertheless, she seemed to be content, although her hands started to atrophy. I massaged them and placed objects in her palms as gently as I could in order to keep them functional. Her fingers curled around the soft, rolled up hand towel that I placed there. Apparently, she continued to have mini strokes, though, so much of my hand therapy was in vain. I suspect that, on some level, the human touch must have been comforting to her, regardless.

As time went by, she began to move less and less, and seldom spoke. I loved to visit her though. I would call her "Granny." When I would leave, I'd kiss her on the cheek. She was one of the darlings of the staff as well. They took very good care of her.

In 2006, on the day of her 95th birthday, I kissed Elise goodbye and told her that I would see her after my three-week vacation overseas. While I was in Israel I dreamt of a beautiful little brown bird that was sitting among blossoms in a cherry tree. I often dream of birds when someone dear to me passes away, so I checked my emails from afar. Sure enough, I had received a message from the head nurse informing me that Elise had peacefully passed away in her sleep.

I prayed for Elise's soul from one of the holiest places on the Earth, not knowing if she had ever been particularly spiritual. I hoped my words would reach her and that, on some level, she was aware of my offering and had now "*flown to the kingdom of immortality.*"*

Tip:

Remember that a gentle touch can be very calming. See if your resident would like you to massage their hands.

Phil

I was Phil's Golden Girl. That's what he called me. It had nothing to do with the color of my hair and I wasn't old enough to look like the characters from the television sitcom of the same name. He told me that it was because I was "pure gold" and that I treated him "like royalty."

Phil did not take well to care home living. He never adjusted to being separated from his wife. I did my best, though, to make some of the time that he was away from her more enjoyable. Like many other couples I've been acquainted with, Phil and his wife had to be separated, due to a lack of moderately priced in-home care. It was an agonizing decision for his wife of 60 years.

At the urging of their now grown children, Phil was put into a private room, in the nicest possible care home. It was a newly built and very modern facility. At a cost of over $30 million dollars, it had all of the latest gear and gadgetry for lifting immobile patients out of their beds. Patients could be transferred in and out of their wheelchairs as well, with ease. Equally important was the fact that a sling and pulley eliminated back related injuries for the care workers. That didn't make it any more pleasing to Phil though. He found it very upsetting to be lifted up above his bed like Peter Pan.

Many times I would find him ranting, but I got him smiling when I asked him things about his past. During these diversionary tactics I found out that he had been quite an artist. For most of his life, Phil had very steady hands. He also had a good eye for neatness and exactness. He had worked as a draftsman. I had seen some of his work at home. Coincidently, I had recently toured the home of a mutual friend and had seen the artwork that Phil had created in their recreation room. It was nice to hear about the things that gave him meaning and purpose.

Phil had many great pleasures from his past. Whenever he would tell me about the days he had spent at the lake, his eyes would light up. He and his wife owned a cabin there and had enjoyed great days of boating, fishing and water skiing. He also liked to fish on the ocean and raved about salmon. He used to say to me, "When I get out of here, we're going to go barbeque a salmon."

It was also his dream to visit the Grand Canyon. He hoped that he and his wife could take me there some day. That never materialized, but we did do other things. In the summer, I brought him a piece of barbequed salmon and fibbed that I had caught it just for him! The following winter, I booked a wheelchair taxi in which we participated in the city lights tour. It's so beautiful during the Christmas season. Our driver took us to some very well lit houses, which thrilled Phil immensely. On the way "home," we stopped and picked up a milkshake. We should have had hot cocoa, given that it was winter, but Phil wanted a milkshake, so that's what I bought for him.

Phil

On more than one occasion, a particularly regimented caregiver said to me that I had ruined Phil's appetite. "Big deal," I grumbled under my breath. He was in his eighties and, with his level of inactivity, he didn't need to consume a huge meal, so I don't think it hurt. His adoring wife was always bringing him healthy snacks and chocolate as well. Of course, I recognize that nutrition is important, but to see him smile when he was given something sweet was so enjoyable!

Cafeteria staff, the janitors, the volunteers in the gift shop, all were extremely cheerful when I would take Phil to the main foyer. They gave him a warm and genuine greeting. In return, he would smile, nod and sometimes salute. This was often followed by a whisper to me in jest, "Everyone knows the monkey. But the monkey knows no one." He must have felt a little bit like a caged monkey himself, at times.

As an unsettled patient, Phil could complain and cry out very loudly. Eventually, it became disturbing for the staff and the other residents, so he was given medication that would "take the edge off." Sadly, out of respect for the other residents and staff, his voice was silenced with sedatives. As a result, he was often pretty doped up and, at times, he would sleep through both breakfast and lunch.

In the first few months of his care home stay, I used to take him to art classes on Fridays where a local artist of some caliber would lead several of the residents in an art therapy lesson. It really evolved and many of the residents who had limited use of their bodies produced some amazing pieces, which decorated the halls at every turn. Unfortunately, Phil's steady hand became shaky with his daily mellowing dose of medication, so he became unable to produce much of anything, except some squiggly lines on the paper.

Initially, his mobility issues had come about as a result of a stroke he had suffered. He deteriorated steadily over a period of months. His adoring wife would visit him daily, unless she was ailing. With their extended medical plan, she was able to arrange for a massage therapist to come in once a week to see her husband. A physiotherapist came in once a month as well.

His physical needs were being met and, spiritually, Phil had a strong faith. Although we came from different religious backgrounds, I had attended enough church services to know some hymns and I put my singing ability to good use.

One day in November, he took a turn for the worse. I stood at his bedside, drawing on that faith and singing the hymns, *Amazing Grace* and *How Great Thou Art*. Despite his labored breathing, I know he knew I was there and I'm sure he was comforted by the lyrics.

That same night, Phil's son called me to say that he thought his father would pull through and make it to see another Christmas. That was not to be. The following morning, upon arrival at the care home, I opened Phil's door to find him still and not breathing. The nurse compassionately informed me that he had passed away peacefully, just before dawn.

Phil

I sat alone with him for a few minutes thinking that he did indeed look peaceful. Unlike when he had first been placed in the care home, I finally felt that, this time, Phil had accepted his new home - a heavenly abode that is known in sacred writings as *"the home of peace and laughter and exaltation."**

Tip:

The radio station should be tuned to whatever station your resident would normally enjoy. Don't leave it tuned to Country & Western if they would prefer to listen to Classical.

Vivienne

Sandy worked in the Activation Department of one of the care homes. It was her job to ensure that all of the residents received stimulation and activity. In her opinion, one of the female residents was not getting enough of either of those things, so she had given my name to this resident's daughter.

Vivienne was a crusty woman with a beautiful smile. She was a former schoolteacher who liked order and respect. Much to the chagrin of the care aids, her favorite thing to yell was "Help!" It was very unsettling because, when you heard her yell out, you were sure that she had fallen on the floor or perhaps into the toilet! I explained to her many times that her behavior was an indication of an emergency and that, it was not an emergency when she needed help in pulling her pants up. Neither was her shear boredom.

When I met her, Vivienne was in her eighties and, as the result of a stroke, she was confined to a wheelchair. She was a divorcee and, according to one of her daughters, the mere mention of her "ex" could evoke a bit of profanity from her mouth. An extremely independent soul, she had looked after her own home and garden, and had driven a car until the date of her stroke.

Many times, she would make her way onto the elevator, and then go down to the lobby to poke around. Although she did that on her own, she didn't like to be alone, so she absolutely beamed when she would see me coming toward her.

Vivienne loved walks, cups of tea, lottery tickets and bingo. She adored a good joke. She also enjoyed seeing her daughters and her grandchildren, all of whom she seemed to have a good rapport with.

Her room was like a snack bar, with open packages of cookies, chips, peppermints and the like. Her decor was mainly photos, plants and a few teddy bears. There was always a well-stocked canister of dog biscuits sitting on her desk so that she could feed her special friend "Kosmo." He belonged to one of her caregivers.

Sometimes, I would read to her from Reader's Digest, mostly from the sections *Life's Like That* or *Kids Say the Darndest Things*. She'd chuckle and tell me some of her teaching career funnies. She liked to tease and be teased. She enjoyed harmless fun and saw humor in many things.

The first summer we met, I spent a lot of time with her over a two-week period because both of her daughters had gone on vacation with their families. It was during this time that we enjoyed a couple of nice take-out meals of fish n' chips. We sat out in the courtyard of the care home and enjoyed the warm sun and fresh air together. Then we moseyed around the garden looking at all of the flora that was coming into bloom. She really liked flowers, both the kind that grow outdoors and the kind that can grow indoors. It gave her great pleasure when people would bring her a plant or a bouquet for her room.

One of Viv's favorite outings was to get me to push her over to the nearby construction site so that she could watch the progress that was being made there. She enjoyed the noise and the action. To be honest, though, what she really liked was to watch the construction workers! Sometimes, when I'd arrive at the care home, she'd already have her coat on and would be gazing longingly out of the window in their direction!

We continued to go outside throughout the autumn season. I'd pick up bright colored leaves for her and she'd hold them in her hand as we went along. When we returned to her room, she'd delight in arranging the leaves in a bouquet and in placing them on her desk in a vase.

Rainy days never bothered us. Viv would want to go out anyway and would wear her rain poncho with its hood pulled over her head. Once, at her request, I pushed her wheelchair straight through a puddle! She got splashed and laughed wholeheartedly! Then she shouted, "DO IT AGAIN!!"

I was Vivienne's companion for two or three winters. During the pre-holiday period, I would write Christmas cards on her behalf. This would include writing something interesting and positive about the past year. Then, she would shakily sign her name. While I was sealing the envelopes and licking the stamps, she'd explain a bit about her relatives and friends. I learned a little about her past and the years that she spent growing up in a small Canadian town.

Each year in late November, Vivienne and I would go to the craft fair that was held in the main foyer of her care home. She always delighted in shopping at the booths and in buying Christmas gifts for her family and their pets.

Craft activities and decorating for special occasions also gave her pleasure and, when she wasn't napping, or visiting her family, or chatting with me, she would join in with the Activity Worker. I would often find her following the worker around, assisting her with Valentine, Easter or Christmas decorating.

The Vivienne I grew to know and love was extremely appreciative. She expressed gratitude for the manicures I did for her and the other little things I did, such as cleaning her jewelry. She liked the pampering and always thanked me. Her quality of life was good, even though she couldn't use her hands very well or walk. She made the most of her somewhat confined existence, right up until the end of her life.

It's hard when people who we're fond of leave us. I wasn't prepared for Vivienne's swift passing. It was truly a sad day when her daughter telephoned me to tell me that her mother had died. I was shocked by the news. Apparently, Vivienne had suffered an agonizing pain while she sat in the dining room. The kitchen staff saw her go limp, and then she slumped over the table. An ambulance was called immediately. However, she died enroute to the hospital as a result of an aortic aneurism.

Vivienne

Vivienne's family included me in a small gathering at the graveyard when they interred her ashes in a mausoleum. Later, I was invited back to one of the homes for a toast. "To Grandma!" they shouted. "To Viv!" I exclaimed.

With my eyes shut, I imagined a leaf falling off of a tree in autumn, caught on the breeze of heavenly bounty, floating gently, gently to the ground.

Tip:

Find seasonal decorations for windows or bulletin boards. Since a lot of time might be spent in bed, it's nice to have a new scene to look at a few times a year. Bright colored leaves in autumn; flowers in spring and summer; fresh holly, cutouts of snowflakes or glittery things in winter.

Liza

Liza was an elderly woman who lived at a care home. Her sons wanted a weekly visitor for her, so they were forwarded my name. They and their families cared deeply for her. They led busy lives, though, and they were happier in the knowledge that, if they went on vacation, or just could not make it in to the care home, at least someone would be visiting their mother regularly.

Liza had aphasia, which is a condition of the brain that often results from a stroke or a head injury. It manifests itself differently, ranging from words that are spoken incorrectly to not being able to speak at all. I surmised that, since she was in a wheelchair, perhaps she had indeed suffered a stroke.

Initially, I found my visits with her to be a bit challenging. We warmed up to each other quickly though, using the language of the heart. We smiled back and forth at one another. Her bright eyes and nods of the head showed me that she understood. A few times, I actually heard her utter some words in her native German language and, occasionally, she tried to say something to me in English. Most of the time, she was keenly aware of what I was saying, so communication wasn't an issue for us. We bonded; we communicated; we laughed.

She did a lot of nodding and beaming when I would point at photographs of her grandchildren. Her family and the staff at the care home informed me that she had been very athletic most of her life. I saw albums that contained pictures of her winning races. There were photos mounted on her wall, of many of the activities in which she had been involved. A sports enthusiast through and through, she had been a hiker, a climber, a biker and a runner.

Liza was in her element when she was outdoors, so I thought it was important to get her out in her wheelchair, rain or shine. I looked forward to our trips around the block. We would stop to smell the flowers and breathe the fresh air. She seemed to enjoy the cars whizzing past, the children walking along the sidewalk with their parents, and all of the other things that we would encounter along our way.

When we stayed indoors, I would throw a soft ball or a balloon at her and she would raise her hands instinctively, and then toss or bat it back to me. Although dementia gets a firm grip and dulls one's faculties, the reflexes seem to be one of the last things to go. That being the case, it was possible for Liza to engage in some light activity. She would smile as she caught what I threw at her, and then look me right in the eye as she threw it back in my direction. Afterward we would enjoy a cup of coffee and a piece of dark chocolate together. Unfortunately, that ritual ended when swallowing became a problem for her, so I substituted solid chocolate for a chocolate meal replacement drink.

Once, when I was leaving the care home, I came across a small, smiling, brown teddy bear on the ground. It was lying directly below Liza's window, which was two floors above. This was at a time when she was a bit more mobile and she could roll her wheelchair on her own and move her arms a little bit. I wondered if she had intentionally pushed the little guy out of the small opening in the window or whether the cleaning staff had accidentally caused his fall. Regardless of how it got there, I put it on the dashboard of my van until my next visit. Both Liza and the bear seemed to share the same contented smirk. Could she have pushed him so that he could try skydiving? If she had, I mused, he most certainly had enjoyed it!

When the limited conversation between Liza and myself ceased completely, our talks became very one-sided, with just nods from her. When those nods ceased, there was only some direct eye contact. Her eyes spoke to me with their gaze. They seemed to have subtle movement and they became brighter when I talked to her. Even on the coldest of days I would bundle her up with an extra blanket on her lap, and with mittens or gloves if I could get her hands to cooperate. Then, off we would go for a walk, looking for some sign of greenery poking up through the frozen ground. She smiled at the crows that had their heads in the garbage and at the dogs that accompanied their owners. When I deliberately put my head in front to look at her, she smiled at me. Her smiles came easily, especially when I did silly things like pirouette around her wheelchair, and take her arm gently and pretend to dance.

Since my primary goal was to uplift her spirit, nourishment came in many forms. It included whispering prayers or poems in her ear, and singing songs to her like *Edelweiss and You Are My Sunshine*. I truly meant it when I would sing the lyrics, *"You make me happy when skies are gray. You'll never know dear, how much I love you. Please don't take my sunshine away."*

During her last days, Liza lay quietly in her bed. Her family members came to be near her. Once or twice, when they left for a bite to eat, or to head home for some rest, I would go in and hold her hand, and say prayers to petition the Creator for a quick and easy passing. I asked that dear Liza's spirit be "refreshed and gladdened."

On the day that she took her last breath, I stood outside her door and imagined that her soul was probably as strong and athletic as her body had been once upon a time. I thought of one of the sentences in a prayer I had read and imagined Liza as a mountain climber looking down upon the Earth from above. I hoped that she was now beholding, *"Thy splendors on the loftiest mount."**

Tip:

Have a sing a long. When out in the garden or walking with a loved one, try to think up some songs you can sing together.

Marney

One day, the care home activity coordinator telephoned to ask if she could pass my name and phone number on to the son of a new resident. Marney was her name. The coordinator was worried about her because she stood by the door a lot in an attempt to "escape" …and make her way back to her former residence. The coordinator was hoping that, if the family would hire me on a regular basis, it would curb Marney's restlessness and confusion.

After some discussion with Marney's devoted and loving son, we decided that I would visit her at least twice each week, during which I would take her for a drive. We also concurred that it would be best to steer her away from her previous residence, literally and figuratively, and then refocus her attention, if that was possible. I discovered that it *was* possible, and she and I warmed up to each other quite quickly.

I explained to Marney that I was a friend of her son's and that, because he was busy at work during the day, he had hired me to take her out for a bit of fun. She was happy about that, but also extremely conscientious that I should be reimbursed for my gasoline. I assured her that it was all taken care of by her son.

During many of those first visits she would ask, "Can you help me dear? I want to go home. Can you give me a ride?" My response was always, "Well, let's go for a drive." Within a few minutes she would forget that she had requested to be driven to her former retirement home and she'd just sit back and enjoy the scenery.

One day, Marney pulled out an envelope with her name and old address on it, and asked me to take her there. I agreed, but I thought to myself that it could be a bit awkward. I knew that the address was that of her former home. Thankfully the staff there greeted her warmly and said that, although they missed her, they hoped she liked her new home. After that day, Marney seldom asked to be taken there. If she did, I found it easy to change the subject.

As weeks turned into months, our friendship grew. The time we spent together was delightful. Although she had dementia, her language skills were still good and conversation was never lacking. Often we would flip through a newspaper or a magazine and discuss fashion because that was something she knew a lot about.

Marney always tried to look her best and her clothing choice was comfortably stylish. Before going out she made sure that her hair was "in place" and her lipstick was "on." From our chats, I discovered where she acquired her acute sense of fashion. She was a former pageant winner and, later in life, she had sat on the board of the pageant selection committee. She had also been employed as a buyer in merchandising, in the fashion department of a large clothing store. Later she owned and ran a successful ladies clothing store. I suspect she was probably born knowing intuitively what goes with what. With her life experience it was natural that she was in style, even in her eighties!

Often, when I went to pick her up, she'd have the television in her room tuned to the golf channel or to the Oprah show. This wasn't really by choice, rather by chance, because she couldn't remember how to operate the television remote. The on/off button was just about all she could manage. For her, the television was familiar companionship.

After putting her coat on and getting a cigarette from the nurse on duty, we'd head out to the patio so Marney could smoke. When she was first admitted to the home, she tried to lean out of the window of her room to smoke. The staff immediately caught her and, for her safety and that of the other residents, her cigarettes were now stored at the nursing station.

Unfortunately, it soon became obvious to me that a chain smoker, named Betty, had Marney in her crosshairs. She would continually bombard Marney with nastiness, while we were outside in the smoking area. Being sweet and unaccustomed to this treatment, Marney tried her best to remain unmoved by the taunts. Nevertheless, Betty was insistent that Marney was wearing a stolen coat.

"Hey," she'd say, "That's my sister's coat. Give it back."

"It's my coat, dear. You're mistaken," was Marney's reply.

This dialogue would usually escalate to, "Hey B****. That's my sister's coat. Take it off!" At that point, I would stand between the two of them and tell Betty to "back off" as nicely as I could. Playing peacekeeper for something so ridiculous was not my idea of fun so, as soon as Marney finished her cigarette, we'd be off for our little drive together.

Many lovely times were spent travelling along a scenic ocean route and, usually, we passed the golf course where Marney had been a long-time member. Sometimes, we'd drive through the neighborhood of her childhood home and she would point it out to me. I heard many interesting stories about her parents and about her upbringing.

Some of her stories were told over and over again. I did a good job of pretending that they were new to me. When the weather cooperated, we'd find a cafe where we could sit outside and continue to chat. I learned about things that had been important to Marney and were still at the core of her being.

She had a strong work ethic, a sense of giving back, of volunteerism and charity, and of maintaining old friendships and connections. She spoke of her dear friend, Lorna, who regularly came to take her out on lunch dates. She was grateful that Lorna kept in touch. Like myself, Lorna overlooked Marney's forgetfulness and took that trip with her down memory lane.

As the weeks and months passed, Marney and I logged a lot of hours together. She either called me "dear" or "Joy." Sometimes, she'd catch herself and say, "That's not your name, is it?" and I'd laugh and say, "No, it isn't. I like the name Joy though. It's okay if you call me that." Once, she said that her daughter's name was Gail and that she certainly would not forget that I had the same name. She certainly did forget it, though, and I went back to being "Joy." I often thought of our car rides together as "Joy rides."

One of the best memories I have of Marney was taking her to a luncheon that was held in her honor. Fifteen years prior, she had founded a women's charity golf tournament and, on this particular day in July, the golf club wanted to pay tribute to her and to the large amount of money that had been raised over the years.

When we arrived at the clubhouse dining hall, she was met with cheers, and showered with accolades and gifts. One gift that really touched her heart was a handmade cushion, which was inscribed with her name and the number of years of service that she had given to the golf club. Although she couldn't remember all of the names of the ladies who were in attendance, she certainly remembered their faces. She was very gracious when she received compliments, handshakes and hugs. Before our departure, many nice photos were taken of her standing beside her cherished golfing partners and fellow fundraisers.

Upon our return to the care home, a much-needed nap was in order and, after I helped to bring in her mementos and "trophies," she settled down on her bed. That day of celebration meant a lot to her and she was thrilled that the staff and the other residents of the care home recognized that her life had meaning and depth.

Summer soon turned to autumn and, on one October evening, Marney's son called to tell me that he was at the emergency ward with her. He said that she had been diagnosed with an aortic aneurysm that had burst. The prognosis was a quick, but painful, death. Quick, meaning that she wasn't expected to live through the night. As I raced to see her in the emergency ward, I paused briefly to speak to a doctor I know who confirmed that Marney wouldn't live much longer.

When I entered her cubicle, I found her conscious, but not wanting to talk. I stroked her hand and she pulled back slightly. I could tell that she really was not in the mood for pity or for speaking of things to come. Basically, she dismissed me. Although, she did manage to give me a slight smile and said, "I'll be alright, dear. You go home." I expressed my love and concern to her and, upon exiting, I prayed silently for her comfort.

The next day, I received amazing news. Marney had made it through the night and was very much alive! In fact, she was overjoyed to see her daughter who had flown in from out of town to be with her. Somehow, the rupture must have repaired itself somewhat and Marney lived on through the week.

With family members coming and going, Marney was well looked after in her final days. I arrived one day to see that a granddaughter had fixed her hair. Another dear companion visited and treated Marney to a nice manicure. She used some colorful polish on her fingernails. "Oh, Marney, you look beautiful," I said. A small smile appeared on her lips and, always gracious, she thanked me.

Marney

It was important for her to look her best, even up to the end of her life and, even more importantly, to have her loved ones at her side. Knowing this, her son and daughter and their families held a bedside vigil, so she was surrounded by love when she passed away. I was sad when I heard the news. However, I was grateful that she had lived longer than anyone had expected.

It was comforting for me to attend Marney's memorial and to join with others in remembering her life. The hall was packed with friends and family, and we were treated to a slide show, which provided proof that she had been very glamorous in her youth. Paramount to this, though, was that her inner beauty shone through. It was evident in the photos of a smiling Marney, as well as in the eulogies and tributes that took place. She had influenced many people through her charity fundraising efforts and through her firm friendships. I surmise that surely she had contentment upon passing, with grace and humility, knowing that she had lived her life well.

I often feel Marney's presence, when I am out shopping for new clothing. I am comforted that I have a fashionista in Heaven who helps me choose designer fashions at a cut-rate price. Since Marney's passing, my sense of what to wear with what has improved. I can only hope that her spirit feels a sense of "Joy."

Tip:

A hair pick and a curling iron can revive a flat hairstyle. Keep these items handy, in a cupboard in the resident's room, or keep them in your vehicle for those quick touchups.

Louise

Dear, sweet Louise. She was suspicious of me from the start. I spent a lot of time yelling in her ear in an attempt to explain the connection between us. Perhaps she thought that I was after her money or that I was a landlord who had come to evict her. Eventually I won her over and gained her trust.

Louise was born in England. She was very astute in some ways. In other ways, she misinterpreted things and came to assume that people were either angry with her or that they were avoiding her.

She suffered from bad hearing, but was compensated for it with good vision, both inner and outer. I found out almost immediately that her hearing loss was not age related. Since childhood, she had been quite deaf in one ear, which isolated her. When I first met her she spent a lot of time in her room reading or playing solitaire.

Her husband had passed away many years before and the children from his first marriage were spread out all over the country. She and her husband had never had any children together so, when her short-term memory started to go, she put herself into a care home. A few years later, the activity coordinator of the senior's residence telephoned me. She was concerned about Louise's solitude and her state of being. I was asked if I could visit her on a regular basis.

Louise

It took no time at all to truly come to love Louise as a dear friend. From day one, I worked on trying to allay her fears. She often felt that she was destitute and that she may end up not being able to pay her rent. She was constantly worried that she could end up living on the street. I assured and reassured her that that would not be the case. She would never be left out in the cold.

After her initial suspicion of me subsided, we got along extremely well together. Of course, like most seniors, she was always worried that she might owe me something for my "trouble." She didn't want to be a freeloader and lived in perpetual fear of not having enough cash.

In reality, a trustee was managing her funds and the care home gave us what we needed from the sundry account. However, within five minutes of receiving it, Louise would always lament about her lack of money. She would say that she had "nothing on her," even if I placed a ten-dollar bill in her pocket. With a reassuring pat on the shoulders, I would remind her that she was solvent and that there was no need for her to worry about finances. However, those assurances were always short lived due to her dementia.

To take her mind off of things, a good walk, a drive or a chat on the beach always brought a smile to her face. Upon returning to her room, I would show her all of the cards and letters that she had tucked away in her drawers. Stockpiled and forgotten. Dozens of greeting cards, which were all addressed to her, proved that many people loved her from afar. She also stored numerous

Louise

photographs in boxes in her room. Some pictures were of her and her husband while they were vacationing together. Others were of bygone days in England with some of her siblings.

Louise had come from a family of six brothers and sisters. She then married a widower who had six children, so she was accustomed to large families and how they are supposed to function. Sadly, her father had not shown his children any love at all and never used that "L" word. She was not her father's favorite and often made that point quite clearly. However, she was resilient nevertheless. She was loved and she knew how to give love.

I'm glad I came into her life and was on the receiving end of her warmth. It became my goal to bring her out of her self-imposed isolation. However, some things were beyond my control, such as when she severed one of the remaining links between her and her stepchildren because she had disconnected her telephone.

To ease her boredom in the evening, I arranged for a loaner television to be brought upstairs. Unfortunately she never turned it on. One of her biggest fears was that she would disturb others, so I bought her a pair of headphones. However, she never got used to wearing them. Louise preferred to read before bed, rather than watch television.

During daylight hours she often watched the seagulls that would sit on the roof outside of her window. Many times when I'd show up for our visit she'd be staring out at them and talking to them like they were her friends. Most afternoons, though, I would find her sitting in a big wooden chair, doling out the cards, playing solitaire or tending to the African violets that sat on her windowsill. She obviously had a green thumb and cared lovingly for these plants, which were displayed in a variety of colors.

It would never take much coaxing to get her to come out with me, though. She would grab her cane, coat and hat and, within five minutes, we'd be out the door. Our drives would often take us past a beautiful Elm tree and the changing seasons would bring different colors to its foliage. That specific Elm was "our" tree and we would comment each and every time I drove past it. We delighted in talking about the new green buds that would appear in the spring, the beauty of the summer, the dying that took place in autumn and the bareness that came with winter.

Another thing that brought Louise a great deal of happiness was seeing little children either playing in the parks, at the beach, in the schoolyard or at the mall. "Oh, bless them," she would comment, in her British accent. Louise adored children, large and small, and she had great insight into parenting. As a stepmother who had parented through the teen years, she told me that the way in which she made kids feel special was to go for a walk with them and just listen.

I often brought my own teens to visit Louise. They were extremely fond of her. In fact, they helped to make her ninetieth birthday a great celebration. My family made a gigantic card for her and I invited some of her former neighbors to an afternoon party, which we held in the meeting room at the care home. We had a large cake and my son played the guitar for her. We all sang

Louise

"Happy Birthday, dear Louise. Happy Birthday to you!!" She was very pleased. But she kept repeating incredulously, "Am I really ninety? I can't believe I'm ninety!"

That huge milestone turned out to be a good way to reach out to some of her friends whom she had lost touch with over the years. One of her dear friends, named Bea, mentioned that she often thought about her but, because Louise no longer had a telephone, it had made it next to impossible to make contact. She was so happy that I had come into Louise's life and that they had been able to reconnect.

After that old friendship was rekindled, I would drive her over to Bea's place for a visit over a cup of tea and, occasionally, the three of us would go out for lunch. It was an absolute pleasure for me and, like so many of the other people I companioned, Louise took pride in dressing up to go on such outings. Her closet was jam packed with many matching skirt-and-jacket combos, as well as dresses, sweaters, scarves and overcoats. She had a shelf full of stylish and unique hats too and she never went anywhere without selecting a felt or wool hat that went well with her outfit. She always chose one that made her look marvelous.

"Madge," she would say when I showed up, "I had hoped you would come today. You're such a good friend." She would often add, "We've had such good times, you and I" and "Do you remember how much fun we had with Kathleen?"

Kathleen was her marvelously fun sister whom she had been so fond of while she was growing up. Madge was a mutual friend of theirs. I never corrected her when she called me "Madge." If it made her happy, it made me happy.

On our way out of the building, we would walk arm-in-arm, passing the nurses, care aids and other residents. She would have something pleasant to say to each one of them, such as, "My that's a lovely shirt you have on, dear" or "You're looking really lovely today." She would shower me with compliments as well. It was great for my ego to hear, "You look fabulous, dear" or "Do you know I love you very much?"

I did know that. I loved her too. We both held a special affection for one another. We were the two members of the "mutual admiration" club and our meetings were held everywhere. We would talk quite loudly, which would interrupt some of the other diners when we were out for lunch. However, when they realized that her deafness was the cause, they would smile at us and resume their own hushed conversation.

On one occasion, we received such nice looks from two male patrons who were sitting nearby that Louise thought they were hitting on us. I told her that it was a compliment to both of us. I jokingly told her that they liked middle-aged ladies and ninety-something ladies, to which she became greatly offended. She was insulted by my comment that she was in her nineties. "INDEED!" An aghast Louise quipped at me. It was obvious that she truly believed that we were both the same age and that she was certainly "nowhere near ninety!" Time flies when a person reaches middle age. It must soar by the time they reach ninety!

Louise

One October evening, the night nurse called to ask me to come and see Louise. Pneumonia had set in to her lungs and she feared that this was the end for her patient. One nasty cold or a flu bug can be the turning point for someone so elderly. By the time I reached her bedside they knew that she was not going to make it much longer. Because none of her family members were around, I stayed with her for most of that evening, and then returned to her bedside in the morning.

Initially, she was aware of my presence and gave me a faint smile. I held her hand and prayed that God, in His continued mercy, would take her quickly and without pain. In a very short amount of time, she was gone, although I sensed that it was painful. As I left, I could hear her voice in my head - words that she often recited, "Good-bye sweet maiden."

As I drove away from the care home, my tears blinded me. My grief quickly turned to happiness though, when I spotted "our" tree. It looked wonderful in its autumn finery! Only a few days earlier, Louise had said to me, "I'm not going to live forever dear and, when I'm gone, you must look at that tree and think of me and know that I love you."

Her love enveloped me at that moment and has done so many times since that day. One of my favorite prayers draws her swiftly to my mind. *"Let the angels of Thy loving-kindness descend successively upon her, and shelter her beneath Thy blessed Tree."**

Louise

After Louise's passing, I found the following in her drawer. It's a typewritten replication of a 17th Century Nun's Prayer:

Lord, Thou knowest better than I know myself, that I am growing older and will someday be old. Keep me from the fatal habit of thinking I must say something on every subject and on every occasion. Release me from craving to straighten out everybody's affairs. Make me thoughtful but not moody; helpful but not bossy. With my vast store of wisdom, it seems a pity not to use it all, but Thou knowest Lord that I want a few friends at the end.

Keep my mind free from the recital of endless details; give me wings to get to the point. Seal my lips on my aches and pains. They are increasing, and love of rehearsing them is becoming sweeter as the years go by. I dare not ask for grace enough to enjoy the tales of others' pains, but help me to endure them with patience.

I dare not ask for improved memory, but for a growing humility and a lessing cocksureness when my memory seems to clash with the memories of others. Teach me the glorious lesson that occasionally I may be mistaken.

Keep me reasonably sweet; I do not want to be a Saint – some of them are so hard to live with – but a sour old person is one of the crowning works of the devil. Give me the ability to see good things in unexpected places, and talents in unexpected people. And, give me, O Lord, the grace to tell them so. AMEN

Louise

The following is a poem I wrote and recited for those in attendance at Louise's memorial celebration…

ODE TO LOUISE

Louise, dear Louise is gone from this place
But rest assured a smile's on her face,
She's happy as a lark, to soar and to sing
A breath of fresh air that blows in the Spring
She can mix with those who she held so dear
And give virtual hugs to those far and near
She's floating on air, she's laughing I'm sure
Her happiness contagious and for it no cure
I miss all our drives and I miss all her hats
Those trips to the beach and those interesting chats
We'd talk about kids and her time as a wife
And she said, "You mustn't be sad when I'm gone from this life."
There's a tree that was "ours" and it's hard to go by
And see it without her to comment "oh my"
A person who showed grace and included some class
When she bade me good-bye "farewell my sweet lass"
Kind words we shall speak when we mention her name
As we would want to be treated exactly the same
Louise is with us in spirit today
let her partake and hear all that we say
No cane will she need at this jolly event
nor will she worry about money that's spent
She won't have to fuss,
And she won't have to pay
Raise your cup in her memory
"Hip Hip Hooray!"

Tip:

Be creative when choosing a night-light. It's nice to bring a cheery light to plug into their outlet for those times when they may need to make their way to the toilet when it's dark.

Jane

Jane and I were neighbors. For fourteen years I had the privilege of living next door to her. During that time she gave me expert gardening advice, showered me with the harvest from what she had planted and put me on the receiving end of her baking.

All of the neighbors loved Jane - children and teenagers alike. Animals loved her too! She was a great source of neighborly information. Rain or shine, she would be out in her garden sharing with folks at some point in the day. We would often wave and shout at each other. Sometimes we would hang over the fence and chat. Many times we would get together for afternoon tea, either at her place or mine.

Over the years, Jane introduced me to her friends, some of whom were locals and some of whom were from overseas. For many years she ran a boarding house. Many of her student boarders would come back and pay her a visit and, when they did, she would be sure to call me over to meet them.

Jane kept an English country garden that was a mix of brambles and deliberate plantings. She knew where everything was planted and the names of everything that was planted there. She kept a logbook of the dates on which she planted things and the dates on which they bloomed.

Jane

Her garden was usually the hub for visitors. In later years, she held court there and friends would stop by, often unannounced. I would watch the comings and goings from my window.

Jane smoked, but only when no one was around. She told me once that she never inhaled. I found that somewhat amusing. She had the "roll your own" type of cigarettes. She kept the cigarette papers in a tin outside. I would watch her roll up the tobacco inside the paper, give it a lick to keep it in there, light it, and then return to her weeding and planting. All the while, that cigarette would be hanging off of her lip. Sometimes she would get caught when a visitor would come through the gate.

One summer her health started to decline. She was extremely tired and seemed to be very distracted. More than once I saw her staring blankly into space. Shortly thereafter, she was diagnosed with geriatric onset diabetes. It was a blood sugar issue, so pricking her finger several times a day in order to get a blood sugar reading became the norm. It was terribly frustrating for her. She was losing weight as well.

A couple of times she shared a bar of chocolate with me. When I inquired about her diabetes and the effect chocolate might have on her, she said, "There's no way I am giving that up!"

Another thing she was "not giving up" was her reading and her thirst for knowledge. She told me that she liked to expand her vocabulary by learning a new word each day. One time she called across the fence to me and asked if I had ever heard of the word *curmudgeonly*. Before I could answer, she explained to me that, basically, it means "a cranky old man being miserly."

In early autumn of that year, Jane was diagnosed with cancer. By Halloween night, she was really not looking well. She had a portable oxygen tank with her at all times. Before my son went out trick-or-treating, he and I went to her place so that she could see him in his costume. She did her best to show interest in his outfit and that meant a lot to him.

Shortly after that visit, Jane was admitted to hospice and, at the end of the first week of November, she succumbed to her illness. Jane had a zest for life up until the very end, living each day fully. She appreciated the little things. She commented on them and was thankful for them.

The family chose to hold her memorial in the Spring. It was a most befitting time for a lady who enjoyed spending so much time in her garden - the perfect time of year for the recollection of a certain someone whose life was so intertwined with the season of renewal. For those who gathered at the memorial, I recited something that I felt Jane imparted to others: "*In the garden of thy heart, plant naught but the rose of love.*"*

Tip:

Bring your children to visit and sing!

Edgar

Edgar was a packer. He had previously lived in Montreal and was determined to return there, so he always had his suitcase ready by the door. I would find him sitting on his bed, or pacing up and down the halls of the care home. As soon as I mentioned that I was taking him out, he'd grab his coat and bag in the expectation that I was taking him to the airport. I'd tell him that we were only going for a ride around town and to leave his belongings in his room. "They'll be safe here," I'd reassure him.

His family had hired me to take him for pleasant diversions because they were concerned about his unhappiness. The first time I took him out he was adamant that we find the "Jewish Store." I took him around and around the city, and up and down the streets looking for it. "No, that's not it!" and "That's not it either!" he grumbled.

That night, I telephoned his daughter-in-law. "Do you know where the Jewish Store is?" I asked. She was just as baffled as I was, but suggested that I try a local bakery that was run by a Jewish couple. The next time Edgar and I went out together I took him there for coffee and a bagel. As pleased as he was, however, that was definitely not the place. Later, we came upon it by chance, while we drove along the main street. "There it is!" he yelled, pointing his finger at Fields Department Store. "What?" I yelled back. "The Jewish Store! Stop!"

Edgar

Fields is known for inexpensive shopping, but I never understood exactly why he referred to it as the "Jewish Store." His daughter-in-law told me that there is a similar place in Montreal where he loved to shop. In any case, I was glad we had located it.

It turned out that all he wanted to buy there were cookies and those cookies got us into trouble! He was stockpiling dozens of them and devouring them in between meals. He existed on little else. The care home offered three nice meals each day. However, on many occasions, he refused to go down to the dining room, so the nurses, his family members and I would ply him with any food that we could. That usually meant giving him a meal supplement drink once a day.

One particular morning I neglected to ask the nurse if he had eaten a good breakfast before I set off with him to shop. As we passed the perfume counter of a local department store, he stopped walking and just stood there. I thought he was just smelling the fragrance but, when I looked at his face, it was ashen and I became scared. Then he wobbled and weaved. I called to a nearby employee, "Help! He's going to faint!"

The lady in the cosmetics department quickly helped me bring him gently to the ground. He was sheepish and angry at the same time. "I'm fine," he kept saying. The store's first-aid attendant had come to look him over anyway.

I was asked if I wanted to have them call an ambulance for Edgar. However, things seemed to improve rapidly as soon as he was given a drink of apple juice and a granola bar, so we declined the offer. In a short time, his condition had improved to such an extent that I decided to continue our shopping mission. I took him to the shoe department and our new friend from the cosmetics department came with us for extra support. Ed selected a pair of sandals and then Lynn (we were now on a first name basis) assisted us to my car.

From that day forward, I always double-checked his food consumption before our departure from his residence. I also started carrying granola bars in my purse to stave off any blood sugar plunges that my clients might have. I wrote a letter to the department store manager praising the efforts of the staff.

After that scare, you'd think I'd be afraid to take Edgar out, but our outings continued. Thanks to his unique disposition and my ability to rebound from whatever came my way, our outings were never dull. My nerves were continually tested by his insistence on telling me how to drive, though. Edgar had been declared legally blind due to his deteriorating peripheral vision. Nevertheless, as a former driving instructor, he insisted on critiquing my parking skills and in directing me as to where to park. It didn't matter if there was a yellow line on the cement to indicate a no-parking zone. He would yell at me anyway.

"There's one. Pull in!"

"Ed, there's not enough room," I would respond firmly.

"Whaddya mean, there's not enough room?" he'd bark. "Stop, for God's sake! You can park there!"

Edgar

My patient, but exasperated, response was "No. I can't, Ed. I'll get a ticket."

On and on it would go. I would circle the block and, eventually, I would find some place that was suitable to park. As I would maneuver my car into the space, he would say things that a driving teacher might say, such as, "Turn your wheel. Turn it. Turn. Okay, straighten, straighten." Knowing full well that he couldn't really see the entire picture, I'd ask, "How am I doing?" and "How does it look?" When I finished parking the car, Ed would compliment me by saying, "Way to go!" Then he would praise me with, "You're quite a girl!"

Being called a "girl" was fun and, often, he would add the name, Sylvia, to that compliment. When I asked his daughter-in-law about that name, she replied, "Oh, he likes you. He really likes you. Sylvia is his ex-wife and he was really fond of her." I didn't have the heart to tell Edgar that I wasn't Sylvia. It was already difficult to tell him I was married to someone else. Although he never tried any moves on me, I didn't want to crush him.

One day, I just happened to be in the city with my husband and our son, so I took them to meet Edgar. We found him sitting on his bed. "Ed, I want you to meet my husband," I said. Then I held my breath, expecting him to give me trouble. He looked my husband up and down, and then looked at me with a smile and said, "Wow, he's a big, big, man!" My husband, who is about five foot nine, towered over Edgar who was only five foot four. I surmised that, because of Edgar's poor eyesight and the fact that he was seated on the bed, my husband must have looked like a giant to him.

In spite of his height, Edgar was bold and assertive. He was emphatic about keeping money in his wallet and about having the freedom to spend it. His sons found themselves in continual conflict with him over his desire to walk around the care home with no less than eighty dollars in his wallet on any given day. They were concerned that he'd lose his wallet.

In order to balance Edgar's need to have cash and his insistence on doing his banking himself, I would take him to his bank once a week. He would rant that he preferred to be taken there on a daily basis. Much to his chagrin, I would escort him up to the wicket and he would admonish me to get the heck out of there!

One day, even though he told me to "SCRAM!" I delayed my departure and quickly handed the teller a note instructing her to give him four five-dollar bills, rather than the four twenty-dollar bills that he always requested. I hoped that, with his confused mind, he would be satisfied with four bills, no matter what their denomination was.

Fortunately, the teller understood that it was not a ransom note and nodded favorably at me. As she carried through this covert operation I held my breath and stood on the sidelines where I could watch and hear what went on. Instead of saying, "Twenty, forty, sixty, and one more makes eighty," she said, "One, two, three... and there, that makes four." At first, Ed looked puzzled.

Edgar

He stared long and hard at the money. Then he took it in his hands and said, "Thank you," with a big beaming smile. We had achieved success. From that day forward, I would wait for that same teller, and then give her a wink. Then the transaction would be completed without a hitch. Getting to know the staff at the bank proved to be lifesaving in the long run.

One cold afternoon, Edgar actually managed to fool a visitor into opening the door of the care home. Then he strode away unnoticed, causing quite a panic. His frightened family looked everywhere for him. I was unaware of his disappearance and was sad that they had not thought to contact me. If I had been notified, I might have suggested that they check the bank. Sure enough, later that day, Edgar's daughter-in-law received a call from the bank manager who said that they had a "cold and tired Edgar" and did they want to pick him up. Edgar and I had become so well known at the bank that, when the very alert staff noticed that I was not with him that day, they became concerned and telephoned his family.

A few months later, when Edgar and I were in that same bank waiting in line, he went completely pale, just like he had when he had fainted in the department store. This time, though, I intuitively felt that something was different. It was as if the hand of death was on his shoulder. As he stared vacantly into space, I said, "Ed, what's wrong? Ed, are you okay?" He didn't answer. I said a prayer under my breath and begged God, "Please don't take him right here." I knew that I would fall apart emotionally if he

108

dropped to the floor. Remarkably, he snapped out of it. I took him out to my vehicle and drove him to the care home immediately.

Upon our return, I relayed the details of the scare to the nurse. She said that she would certainly keep an eye on him. I stayed with him for a while and, because he had perked up, I suggested that he might like to have a haircut at the in-house salon. He agreed.

After his trim, Ed caught a glance of himself in the mirror and smiled. He then smiled at the hairdresser, giving her his full approval for a job well done. There was color in his face again, and he looked tidy and clean-shaven, so I escorted him back to his room. As I departed we exchanged our usual dialogue.

"Bye, Ed. I'll see you tomorrow."

"Yeah kid, if I'm still here. Because..."

I interrupted, "Yeah, yeah. I know, I know. If you're not in Montreal."

"That's your dream - to get back to Montreal."

"Yup," he said.

I turned and walked down the hall toward the elevator.

Ed died that night. I received word in the morning that he had some sort of choking fit and a subsequent heart-related problem. A friend of his family had telephoned to deliver the news. She relayed that, since his family was out of the country, a friend from the synagogue had been at the hospital with Edgar when he passed away. I cried upon hearing the news!

Edgar

Edgar had left this world just a few weeks shy of his ninetieth birthday. A big birthday party had been in the works for him. His family was planning to work on it as soon as they returned from Europe. But, alas, there was no birthday party. There was a rebirth of sorts, though, into the next world.

As we walked through the cemetery to his final resting place, the members of the Jewish community had to console me. It was a somber event of ritual and prayer, and scripture in Hebrew, with the rabbi leading the procession of some thirty or forty friends and family. (There would have been more if it had taken place in Montreal!)

Edgar's burial space was a cavernous hole (I heard a whisper that a huge boulder had to be moved to create it). As they lowered his plain casket, I could hear his voice speaking words of pride, "That's a big, big, hole!"

Although he was small in stature, I knew he was happy that he had one of the biggest resting places in the entire cemetery. God Bless Eddie! Masel tov! Free at last!

Tip:

Men like to carry a wallet; women like to carry a purse. Keep cash amounts minimal and, instead of credit cards, put photos inside for them to look at.

Annie

I didn't have the opportunity to spend a lot of time with Annie because of her health challenges. However, the one morning a week that I did have with her was good quality time. The weather usually cooperated, so a nice walk to the local coffee shop and back, with me pushing her in her wheelchair, was often the order of the day.

Annie's mind was keen. She loved good conversation, which we shared over a cup of coffee and a pastry. Being extremely sociable, she interacted well with the counter staff and the other people in the coffee shop. She had a special charm and a loveable nature, and it was fun to be in her company. The staff at the care home was just as fond of her and, in turn, she praised them. It was important to her that everyone was introduced as her friend.

When we weren't out walking or sipping coffee together, we'd spend time in the lobby of her care residence and enjoy whatever the moment would bring our way. If the mood hit us, we'd sing a few songs or read aloud to one another. Humor was part of every meeting and her laughter was infectious!

During one of the last times we spent together, an especially funny thing happened. When I arrived that day, Annie was eager to show me an innocent looking, ceramic, hound dog that was sitting on top of the television in the common area of her

113

care home. When she turned it over, I noticed that, despite its angelic appearance, it had anatomically correct maleness sticking out of its sheath! Being fairly quick-witted, I uttered a response that my three-year old daughter had blurted out when she saw a live dog in the same position. "Oh, the lipstick is out of the case!" I exclaimed enthusiastically.

Annie nearly fell out of her wheelchair when she heard that. She laughed so hard! She repeated it over and over, and then roared with laughter. It was a little wicked, but it is one of the things that sticks out in my mind, if you'll pardon the pun.

It wasn't all fun and games with Annie, though, because her health declined rapidly. I think her kidneys were shutting down, among other things. She also developed a nasty wound on her elbow that didn't want to heal. Perhaps she had MRSA, which is a terrible antibiotic-resistant staph infection that can claim people in a short period of time.

Doctors don't generally make house calls in this day and age but, when the nurse called Annie's doctor, he came to the care home right away. Annie expressed extreme gratitude to him as soon as he arrived to see her. I was with her at the time. As he removed the dressing and dealt with the lesion, I said silent prayers under my breath. I know it was painful because Annie moaned and groaned. Despite this, when he finished she was pleasant and appreciative to both the doctor and to myself. When I left her that morning I hoped that my sincere petitioning to the Creator helped to lesson her pain.

Annie

Annie passed away in her sleep a day or two later. The morning care nurse found her lying in bed. I wasn't there to comfort her in those last few minutes of life, but I fondly thought back on the warmth we shared over the months.

At her funeral, I sat beside a gentleman I didn't know. We struck up a quiet conversation and, as we chatted and introduced ourselves, I realized that he was the father of a friend of mine. The very next day, I ran into him again at a dinner party. We really laughed. Then, we both said at the same time, "What are the chances?" We agreed that it is a small world. I couldn't help but think that our meeting was not a coincidence. For some reason, Annie thought that we should get to know one another and, from her world to ours, she orchestrated the bond of mutual friendship. That familiar children's song comes to mind when I think of her...

"Make new friends, but keep the old. One is silver and the other gold..."

Tip:

Make Valentines together. You can do the cutting and they can tell you what to write inside. Or address Christmas cards together.

Mark

One day, I described what I do for a living to my daughter's orthodontist. He was very interested in what a paid companion for the elderly does and, during my next visit to him, he broached the subject again. He mentioned that his father, Mark, was nearly ninety years of age. The old gentleman was frustrated with his energy level and extremely discouraged with his inability to walk any great distance. He said that he had explained to his father that it is normal for a man of his age to slow down somewhat. However, regardless of his attempts to appease him, Mark remained frustrated and very discouraged.

"Do you by any chance have any time to spend with my Dad?" I was asked. "I'd appreciate it if you could visit him once or twice a week, and take him out for a walk." I responded, "Hey, in my line of work, openings in my schedule can occur quite suddenly. I'll let you know."

It wasn't long after that when Mark became one of my clients. He was a very tall man and I looked way up to talk to him. His hearing and eyesight were pretty good but, as his son had told me, Mark was not very steady on his feet. I encouraged him to use his walker at all times because, with my little frame, there was no way that I could even hope to support him if he toppled.

Many elderly people who have suffered a fall or two lose their confidence. Mark was no exception, so I chose to use the positive thinking strategy. I warned him that, if he kept telling himself that he was old and doddery, and that he was going to fall, his mind would soon believe it.

"Every day, you have to tell yourself, 'I can do it,'" I said. Then I added, "Look ahead of you, not down at your toes. Hold onto your walker and steady as she goes."

We managed to walk around the garden at his retirement home a few times. We stopped every few feet for a rest and, occasionally, we sat down on a bench. All the while he would be saying things like, "I don't know what's wrong with me, dear. It's very frustrating."

I'd reassure him with, "You're doing fine, Mark," and again I would say, "You're doing just fine."

Sometimes I'd take him away from his residence in my car. Once or twice I drove him past the nearby college and university, and along some roads near where he used to live. He proudly pointed at the house where he and his wife had raised their family. Mark enjoyed citing the accomplishments of his two sons and their wives, and his grandchildren. He knew who was attending college and who had completed what subjects. I didn't mind that there was some repetition of stories and events, and always acted like it was all brand new information to me.

It was only a few months into our friendship when Mark became very weak. No prompting could get him to walk. He preferred to just lie in bed. One of the nurses felt that, perhaps, he was having some TIA's (mini strokes). At this point, I just

Mark

continued my visits with him at his bedside. I would read aloud from the local newspaper and give him sips of liquids if he seemed parched.

One morning, when I came in to see him, I noticed that a lady was playing an electric organ in the main foyer of the care home. The hymn-like music was being carried down the hall and was drifting into his room.

"Hi Grace," he said when I walked in.

(I kind of liked being called Grace.)

"Have you come to take me to church?"

"Well, we could go listen to the hymns if you want to," I replied.

I didn't tell him that the hymn music he heard wasn't coming from a church.

"Yes. I can get up. I can go to church."

He made a move to get up from the bed, but he just couldn't do it.

"Don't worry, Mark. You can stay in here."

"But I want to go to church," he said again. Then he added, "I think it is very important."

"Would you like me to say a prayer with you and maybe sing some hymns?" I offered.

"Yes," he said, "That would be nice."

As he drifted off, I began to say the Lord's Prayer aloud. I followed it by singing, *"Amazing Grace."*

Mark

The next day, his family started holding vigil at his bedside and, in a day or two, he was gone. I thought of him fondly when I received the news. Even though we hadn't known each other very long, we had enriched each other's lives.

When I told Mark's son about my final visit with his father, I relayed the story of how his dad felt the need to go to church during those last days.

"Are you sure that's what he was saying?" his son asked, "Dad was never a church-going man."

"Oh. I am sure," I said, "Really sure."

I thought to myself that, at the end of his life, Mark had felt that need. The words of Amazing Grace perhaps sum it up so well. *"'Twas Grace that taught my heart to fear and Grace my fears relieved. How precious did that Grace appear, the hour I first believed."*

Tip:

Take an atlas or a world map with you. During your visit see if your resident can show you the places they have lived and the places they have travelled.

Trina

Being a companion to the elderly has been rewarding and enlightening and sometimes emotionally exhausting. One year I attended eleven funerals! I remember telling someone that it was like losing your grandmother every month. Some of the people I visited and entertained were in and out of my life very quickly. I would just get to know them, and then they would take a turn for the worse. Believe me, it was nothing I did that sent them to their deathbed! It was just their time. Others, I had the bounty of visiting for many years. One of those people was Trina.

I met Trina about seven years before she passed away. We had many, many joyful times! When I first met her, though, it was a different story. She was absolutely despondent, sleeping a lot and refusing to eat. She was always lying down, facing the wall. When she wasn't sleeping, she was anxious and fretful. I began to coax her to eat and, after her small meals, I would take her out for walks in the sunshine. She and I soon became friends and, after just a few visits, the result was a calmer Trina.

It was no wonder that she had been out-of-sorts initially. Her apartment had been damaged by fire and she had lost many personal possessions. It seemed that, after the fire, her health challenges mounted, so her son and his wife made the decision to relocate her thousands of miles. No longer separated by distance, her family was happy that she would be close to them in her final years. However, she was moved from her town in the east, where she had lots of friends and social connections, to a city in the west where she only knew three people.

At the request of the social worker, I began visiting Trina when she was a patient in the hospital. Subsequently, the family arranged for me to continue the visits after she was placed in a care facility. Of course, I would like to think that it was just because I was her paid companion that she began to improve emotionally. In reality, though, I think that she must have been prescribed anti-depressants because she snapped out of her funk rather abruptly, and then became quite anxious to get out of the hospital. No longer did I find her lying on her bed when I entered her room, rather, she'd be waiting at the door, desperate to get out of the building.

A couple of times she threatened the staff by telling them that she was going to "call the cops!" Although her family told her that the care home was the best place for her, she often felt that she was being held there against her will.

Thankfully, Trina's anxiety eventually gave way to the sweetest and mellowest disposition. She became a darling of the nurses. Her blue eyes sparkled and her smile shone at every kind word that came her way.

She and I never had long engaging conversations, but the few words we did exchange were meaningful. She always smiled for me and her eyes would light up, especially when something was humorous, or when she saw dogs or babies!

Trina

For the first year or so, Trina didn't have a television in her room. She said that she didn't want one. However, after a couple of nasty falls, she began to have more and more "in-bed" days. One time, it was because of her arm; another time, it was because of her hip. Consequently, she would spend long hours in bed.

At that point, I insisted on getting her a television. I found one that we could borrow. It was a loaner that was kept in the storage room of the care home. I made sure that the staff knew to keep it tuned to the TLC channel, which is the channel that features lots of babies! Alternatively, if there weren't any programs that featured little ones, the staff knew to change the channel to something that pertained to animals. Occasionally, I would come in to see her and she would be watching a hockey game or a curling match on her television. It turned out that she was quite an enthusiastic armchair (wheelchair!) sports fan.

The television really held Trina's interest - until I walked in the door. It was apparent that she would rather visit with me, so I'd hit the "off" button. Instead, if she were having an "in-bed" day, we'd look at her hometown newspaper. Her sister had paid for her to have a subscription. It was nice to read the articles to Trina. She would point at photos of her friends that she recognized.

On fair weather days, if Trina was out of her bed, we'd go for a stroll in the garden. She would delight in all of the beauty of the season. In the summer, she especially liked me to push her wheelchair as close as I could to the flowers so that she could lean over and smell their fragrance. Her favorites were the sweet scented roses.

During the rainy days of autumn, we would keep company by enjoying a cup of tea in the dining room, or by listening to the music of solo entertainers, musical duos, choirs and groups of children. Our time was also spent in the gift shop, seeing what items had arrived and, occasionally, making a purchase, such as a cuddly teddy bear that would sit on her bed.

I sometimes wrote letters to her friends "back home" on her behalf. Before mailing them, I would read them out to Trina for her nod of approval.

Trina

Dear Ladies,

Thank you so much for your recent letter to Trina! It sure put a smile on her face when I read it to her. She loves to receive letters from "back home" and especially from her dear friends at the Legion.

Her sister brings her the Eganville and Renfrew County newspapers and I go through them with Trina page by page looking for familiar faces.

It would be wonderful if you could send a recent photo of the Ladies of the Legion. Perhaps a picture taken at your annual Honors and Awards night?

I will be sure and put it up on her wall so she can look at it often!

Trina is well cared for. She has a nice room on the top floor of one of Victoria's newest care facilities. She has been here since it opened three years ago, and seems to be settled.

At the request of Trina's son and daughter-in-law, I visit Trina at least once per week and have become good friends with her over the past few years. Her speech isn't good enough to carry on a conversation but she would want you to know that she thinks of you fondly and often.

Sincerely,
Gail (on behalf of Trina)

Trina

In November, there were two activities that we looked forward to enjoying together - the Veteran's Day ceremony and the winter craft sale. Trina always had some spending money and we would make purchases for her "granddogs" and families. Since she had no grandchildren, she spoiled her son's dogs rotten! We bought Christmas wreaths for her special pets, which were made out of dog treats, and anything else she fancied.

The years went by, and then, in April, just a few days after we celebrated her 89th birthday, Trina's health started to rapidly decline. She ate very little and began losing weight. I tried coaxing her with various types of soft food. I took a lot of time encouraging her to swallow before she took the next bite. It was not a pleasant existence. In fact, it was quite an ordeal for her and her eyes said as much to me. True to her good nature, she still managed a smile or two, a faint whisper of a compliment, and added quietly, "Thanks."

One sunny day in May, I walked into her room and was shocked to see how thin she had become and how her face had changed. The nurses and I figured that she must have had a stroke. Something told me that this might be our last visit together, so I took her out to the garden in her wheelchair. I showed her all her favorite flowers. I commented that, soon, her favorite rose bush would be in bloom.

When we came back indoors, I telephoned Trina's sister and put the receiver up to her ear so she could listen to the sound of her sister's voice. Although the conversation was one-sided, she did manage a hint of a smile as she listened to her sister's words.

Trina

When I hung up the receiver, I took her into the care home chapel and recited the Lord's Prayer aloud. It was just she and I alone in there, and the acoustics were good and I found myself singing, "All things bright and beautiful; all creatures great and small; all things wise and wonderful. The lord God made them all."

When I returned her to her room, she had a smile on her face. I told her how much she was loved by her sister, and by her son, his wife and their dogs... and also by me! I kissed her on the forehead and waved good-bye to her, saying, "See you soon Trina!" However, my dear Trina passed away the following afternoon.

I thought I would see her soon, to sit at her bedside. I didn't expect her to leave so quickly! I was told that she shut her eyes contentedly and slipped away. It's the way most of us hope to go when our time comes. In reflection, I was glad that I had done all the "right" things just the day before.

It wasn't long after her passing that I received a nice card in the mail from her son and her daughter-in-law. They thanked me for the wonderful friendship that had blossomed. They said that I had brought their mother great happiness and much comfort to them, as well. I added it to the stack of cards they had written me over the years. That was when I came across the following note of appreciation, which had been written at the beginning of our friendship:

"Just a note to say thanks again for everything. You sure put a smile on Mom's face! She is very content and happy now at her care home. We appreciate everything you have done!" I smiled as I looked at those words, feeling with certainty that she still felt very happy and content now, in the rose garden of paradise.

Tip:

Leave a note taped to the TV with favorite TV channels listed. There's no point in having the television tuned into the sports channel if the resident is a fan of cooking programs. If resident is hard of hearing be sure and have the text scrolling on screen. Purchase some headphones if necessary.

Colleen

Colleen was not one of my clients. We were simply friends. Although we were miles apart in age, we had a good camaraderie. She was a relatively carefree divorcee who had adult children. I was a married woman with young children.

Colleen saw beauty in everything and never took anything in nature for granted. Each summer she would go to a secluded beach, towing her little trailer behind her. She would stay there for a few weeks, all on her own. She was quite thrifty and her needs were simple. As long as she had a bit of food, a thermos of hot coffee, a morsel of chocolate and a book to read, she was absolutely in Heaven.

Even though she had a driver's license and owned her own car, she would telephone me every autumn, to see if I could pick her up and take her for a drive. She liked me to be her chauffeur so that she could drink in the sights of the trees turning color. The leaves in their splendor had Colleen squealing with delight at every new stretch of road.

Sometimes, in the winter, we would just call each other up and comment on the weather.

Colleen would say, "Brrr. Isn't it cold today?"

I would answer, "Nasty weather."

"Gotta get away from here," she would say. Then, she would add, "I've planned a trip and am heading off by bus to Arizona," (or Mexico, or some other hot, dry place).

Colleen didn't have a huge income and I don't think she got a penny from her ex. But she had been awarded the house in the divorce settlement. She had worked hard selling cosmetics, so she was able to manage financially on some sort of a pension, as well as on an inheritance from a relative. She did make it a priority to have enough money to travel and, every winter, she would go somewhere. Upon her return, she would call to tell me about her journey, detailing all the fabulous sights she had seen.

Once, and only once, she asked me to go abroad with her. She knew that I had young children, so she was hesitant to ask. But, nevertheless, she did call me up to ask if I would be interested in going to Thailand and Bali with her. I said that it sounding tempting, but that I just couldn't manage it. I was tickled that she thought of me as a good enough friend to invite on a trip, especially since she was so independent.

Not long after her return, Colleen suffered a bad fall. She was taking her groceries up to the cashier at the grocery store when she stepped on a candy Lifesaver that someone had dropped on the floor. She took a huge tumble! She said, "I slipped on my arse!" and then, acknowledging the irony of having slipped on a LIFESAVER, she added, "It's not funny!" It was obvious she was in excruciating pain and, in retrospect, she should have asked the store manager to call an ambulance for her. Instead, she made her way back out to her car. She was embarrassed and probably in shock.

It turned out that she had suffered a broken pelvis. She recounted to me that she never knew how many daily actions are connected to one's pelvis. Every movement or gesture, every laugh or grimace, hurt her terribly. I visited her often during this time and, when she was mobile again, she had to deal with a number of problems. Within a couple of weeks, she went from an initial diagnosis of osteoporosis, to having full-blown pneumonia. It was one thing after another. Eventually, she was diagnosed with lung cancer. Her furrowed face attested to the fact that she had once been a smoker. But she had given it up some years before. Alas, it was too late.

One sunny afternoon in late August, we went walking along the waterway, albeit slowly. She drank in the beauty of the place and the majesty of the moment that we were experiencing. She certainly didn't want to talk about death or funerals. When I tried to broach the subject gently, she would have nothing of it. She was a spiritual person and had incredible spirit. There was so much more of her life here on Earth that she still wanted to experience.

I asked her about her plans for her upcoming birthday in September.

"What would you like to do?" I queried.

"I know what I DON'T want to do," was her reply, "I don't want to celebrate with our mutual friend this year."

Colleen

Our friend's dog shared her birth date and, although it had been a great joke at one time, this particular year, she made it clear that she wanted a celebration just for herself.

Autumn came and the leaves put on a brilliant show. Unfortunately, this particular year, Colleen could only see them from her hospital bed. I visited her one November day and her breathing was labored. She was drifting in and out of a deep, morphine-induced sleep.

I plugged in the portable CD player, which I had brought with me, and hit the PLAY button. When she heard the distinct sound of harp strings being plucked, Colleen opened her eyes with a surprised look. I laughed when I realized what must be going through her head. Then I said, "Relax, Colleen. You're not in Heaven yet!" She smiled a big smile and relaxed blissfully. If the tales are true of angels playing harps at the Pearly Gates, at that moment, she surely must have thought that she had arrived!

As I sit here recalling Colleen's life and the end of it, I realize that this is a most suitable day for writing about her. With the memory of her sparkling eyes and her immense smile, and her Irish lilt, I remember that today is St. Patrick's Day. Did she have the luck of the Irish? It seemed to me that her dying went on for days. I begged God to end her suffering and take her. I came and went. Yet, each time I came to her bedside, she was still alive.

One evening, I stayed at the hospital until nearly midnight. The moment seemed to be close. She was gasping and railing and yet, she wouldn't go. I whispered in her ear, over and over, that it was okay to leave. Then it dawned on me - Colleen was too independent. She liked to travel alone. She didn't need me with her. She was going solo.

I went outside and said to the nurse on duty, "I'm going to leave now. She needs to be on her own. Some people need others to be with them and some don't. This is Colleen's journey and I sense that she doesn't want me here."

The next day, I telephoned the hospital and found out that Colleen had departed a short time after I had left her bedside. Immediately upon hearing the news, the following Gaelic Blessing came into my mind...

"May the road rise to meet you. May the wind be always on your back. May the Sun shine warm upon your face; the rains fall softly on your fields. And until we meet again, until we meet again, may God hold you in the palm of His hand."

Tip:

Bring soothing music and a device with which to play it

Kit

I visited Kit for at least five years. When she and her husband first moved into the nursing home, she already had considerable dementia. It didn't stop her from carrying on a first-rate conversation though. She was extremely interesting and had a lot of stories to tell about her past. Born in Finland, but raised in Canada since the age of two, she had led a very busy, fun life.

Kit's family wanted her to get out as much as possible. Her husband was extremely attentive and sharp, but he was in a wheelchair, so he was limited in what he could do. Sometimes their daughter would arrange a wheelchair taxi service for her parents, or she would book them on the local wheelchair bus service, and then meet them at a local shopping mall or bring them to her house.

At least twice a week I would take Kit out for a drive. We would usually start by buying her absolute favorite treat - a chocolate ice cream cone. Then we would head to the waterfront, and sit and enjoy it.

Kit had been an excellent baker and those who were close to her told me about her fabulous homemade bread and cinnamon buns. She had also been a cake decorator and showed me many photos of her birthday and wedding cake creations. She had been quite a prolific painter too! Her family had brought her art into the care home and the staff had hung it in the halls for all to view. It was during those times when we ate ice cream that she would tell me about the "good old days."

One day, as we were finishing up our drive, I asked her if she would like me to buy her a coffee with which to wash down her ice cream. She replied, "Why would I want to get such a wonderful taste out of my mouth?" Then she added, "Why ruin a good thing?!" A lady after my own heart, she wanted to savor the taste of the chocolate as long as she could!

Kit's mobility progressively worsened, however, and she began to become confused as to how to get in and out of my vehicle. It became impossible for me to coach her on how to get out of her wheelchair and into my car. I didn't want to injure myself attempting to transfer her so, instead, we resorted to staying at the care home for our visits.

One way to stimulate her mind and keep her busy was to have a spelling bee. Boy, could she spell - even with her dementia! If people walked by when I was quizzing her, they were always very impressed. Obscure words were not a problem for her to spell and, occasionally, I would throw in the easy ones. Those who passed by would hear her loudly spelling "I-C-E C-R-E-A-M" or "M-I-S-S-I-S-S-I-P-P-I."

If we weren't engaged in spelling, we'd often be singing. Kit could carry a tune very well and remembered most of the words to a lot of songs. We would sing wartime songs, country songs and pop songs. I would start with the opening lines, and then she would finish the song.

Kit

Kit did go through a period of considerable angst and, when she didn't have someone with her, she would call out continually. It was then that her family doctor agreed to put her on some types of medication that quelled her agitation. However, until he got the dosage right for her, it seemed to have the opposite reaction. Her constant, "Hello. Hello. Hello," which grew louder and louder, in addition to the sound of her hand tapping on the side of her chair, upset the other residents and added to the stress levels of the staff. That was when I came up with the idea to get her a portable CD player (a cheap option to the not yet mass produced iPods). I popped in a Golden Oldies CD and put headphones on her head.

Within a few minutes, she forgot her mantra and replaced it with the words to her favorite songs. There was one song, in particular, that she would sing along with at the top of her lungs. It was that Roger Miller 1960's classic, "*King of the Road.*" You could hear her belting out "*Trailer for sale or rent, rooms to let fifty cents, I am a man of means by no means… King of the road!!*" It was indeed a hit with her and also with the staff who were elated that they could now keep her calm and occupied for longer periods of time.

I couldn't do as much with her anymore, though. She slept more often and suffered some rough times with recurrent health issues. Her steadfast husband, Chuck, was an absolute hero in my eyes. He was always concerned about his wife. I would accompany them to concerts at the care home, during which they would hold hands. Sometimes Kit became really confused and she'd announce that Chuck was not her husband. I know that hurt him initially. Later, he saw the humor in it and asked her, "Kit, if I am not the man who has been married to you for over fifty years, who am I then?" She would giggle in embarrassment.

Although they had separate beds, they were lucky enough to share a bedroom at the care home. Mementos and photos adorned the shelves and the walls of that room. Fishing trips, grandchildren, dance hall parties and anniversary cards spoke of good times past and a wonderful marriage. Every Saturday night, Chuck would watch re-runs of the Lawrence Welk show on the television in their room. He told me how he missed the music and how he missed dancing with Kit.

Surprisingly, it was Chuck who left this world first. He died just a few days after his 92nd birthday. His mind was as sharp as a tack and, in some ways, it didn't seem fair. Do we get a choice in that matter, though?

A day or two after he died, Kit got a new roommate. The person who slept in Chuck's old bed was a lady with a lovely, caring smile. She took a great interest in Kit's well being. Shortly after she moved in, I offered to read her horoscope out of the newspaper. "I'm think I'm Aquarius," she stated. "My birthday is February 2nd." The hair on the back of my neck stood up! She had the exact same birth date as Chuck! Not only was her birthday on the same day, but she had just turned 92 years old as well!! They had the exact same birth year too!! I don't believe in reincarnation, but I do believe in signs of love from the Great Beyond - signs that say, "Please don't forget me. I am still here to take care of you!" Had Kit's husband somehow orchestrated this scenario?

One evening, shortly thereafter, I tuned into the Lawrence Welk re-runs. It brought a smile to my face when the host sang, *"Here's a song and a prayer that every dream comes true, from now till we meet again... adios, au revoir, aufwiedersehn."*

Kit lived another few months after her husband's death. Sometimes, she called out his name and her roommate would assure her that she would see him soon. Eventually, Kit slipped away in her sleep. I think Chuck was waiting for her with outstretched arms and, surely, she would have recognized him. There would be no fog and no confusion - just a choir of angels belting out *"King of the Road"* as their souls danced!

Tip:

Exercise the mind: Have a spelling contest.

Jean

As Jean would say, "Get on with it"! That's the way she felt and she spoke her mind, especially if we were waiting for a musical concert to begin. She was impatient, so she would attempt to take charge when the musicians were tuning up their instruments, or when the nurse's aids and activity assistants were wheeling the other residents and patients in to the music hall. She would indicate loudly that it was time to start the show.

When I met her years before, Jean had a lot more patience. We had connected through a mutual friend - a British chap who was in both the English Speaking Union and the Monarchist League. He took me to a luncheon. It was there that I was first introduced to her.

At that time, Jean was a demure and fashionably dressed elderly lady. Although the passage of time may have taken away her demure, she remained a smart dresser well into her nineties. Her favorite color was red and it wasn't hard to miss her when she went out shopping in her red suit or when she was flitting around town in her bright red car.

Somehow we lost touch for a while. Then, when I was visiting at the local hospital, providence brought us back together. There was Jean, lying in one of the beds. She had suffered a stroke and was waiting to be placed in one of the care homes. She expressed disappointed that she was no longer driving her snazzy red car, but was now going to have to be content in a wheelchair. She still had her marvelous sense of humor, though, and she was keenly interested in what I had been up to. I promised her that we would get together as soon as she took up residence in her new digs. At that time, she was 95 years of age.

A short time later, Jean's daughter telephoned me to ask if she could pay me to keep visiting her mother. I felt rather guilty about charging an old friend for my services but, in the end, I agreed that I would - at a reduced rate.

Those visits with Jean usually included getting a breath of fresh air. She delighted at my pushing her around the block or down to the local shopping mall. Another ninety-something friend of hers lived right next door and, a couple of times, I managed to get the two of them together for afternoon tea.

Many times, Jean and I would just sit on the deck of her care home and gaze upon the busy street below, listening to the birds above the traffic noise, or filling each other in on current events. It didn't matter what we were doing, as long as we were together. If I wasn't there, inevitably, Jean, the sun worshipper, would be soaking up the rays. She always had a book on the go or a newspaper folded on her lap. It was her goal to keep her mind active right to the end.

When my visits went on longer than an hour, she would try to be diplomatic and say, "Now listen, darling, I don't want you to stay too long. I'm sure you have so many things to do." I always reassured her that it was my pleasure to spend part of my day in her company and that I would leave before rush hour traffic appeared on the roads.

One day, just before I was departing, she pointed her finger at a ceramic donkey, which was attached to a ceramic, flower-filled wheelbarrow.

"I'm getting one of those when I die," she said.

"What? A ceramic donkey?" I queried.

"No," she said, "A real one."

"Really?!" I laughed.

She went on to say, "Yes. All my life I have wanted a donkey and God told me that I can have one when I leave this world."

I blurted out, "Oh, how fun!" and "Do you want that in your obituary? I could make sure that your daughter writes that you finally got your donkey."

She smirked and said, "Yes. Absolutely. Make sure everyone knows."

Shortly after her birthday the following spring, Jean took ill. Within days, she went from being high functioning to being completely bedridden. I popped in to see her. It was apparent that she really didn't feel much like visiting. There was no red lipstick on her lips, no rhinestone, cats-eye glasses hanging from a chain around her neck and no travel brochure lying open beside her in display of some far away destination.

Jean

I stood at the door and blew her a kiss. She gave me a withered look, and then managed a smile when I said, "I love you, Jean. Get well soon." She replied, "I love you too darling."

Over the next few days, nieces and nephews, brother and sister-in-law and, of course, doting daughter and granddaughter, all came to see her. At one point, she rallied and told them not to fuss. Then she opened her eyes and said crustily, "I am not dead yet!" They burst out laughing, realizing that she had taken exception to the type of music they were playing on the CD player. First they played Patsy Cline songs, and then they had moved to an instrumental and somber genre of music that resembled a funeral march! Then they wisely decided to replace that with the soundtrack from the movie *"The Sound of Music."* When Jean did exhale her final breath, it was during the very last stanza of one of her all-time favorite songs, *"Climb Every Mountain!"*

Many people who eulogized Jean at her memorial spoke of her kindness, compassion, generosity and love. While she didn't always have patience with her fellow seniors who were in wheelchairs or with the musicians who were tuning up, she had an enormous amount of patience and understanding for those who had special needs. She always had a soft touch and a kind word for those who were less fortunate than herself.

I gave a brief talk at her celebration of life, and then I sat and listened, while her granddaughter's husband kept his promise to Jean. She had asked him to sing "her" special song and he did.

Jean

He sang, *"Climb every mountain, ford every stream, follow every rainbow, till you find your dream."*

My mind wandered back to the conversation I'd had with Jean about her donkey. I mused about those creatures. They're cute, but stubborn. I had read somewhere that, in the Middle East, they were used to run wells and get water from the ground. They are relatively small animals, but they are accustomed to carrying large loads. Those who have owned them say they represent true loyalty and hard work. Donkeys are sure-footed creatures and I understand that they do not follow blindly. If they are unsure, they will simply not move. They're not dumb animals; they're actually very smart.

Could that be why Jean wanted one? Did she indeed have her very own donkey now? Was I reading too much into this? Was I thinking too much about Jean and her love of donkeys? It was then that I heard her voice in my mind. "Get on with it!", she said, a tad bit irritated.

Tip:

Sit together at a piano and see if you can play a duet. Maybe your resident can read sheet music. It may be a surprise to find out that they can play jazz! Perhaps their fingers will know exactly where to go on the keyboard and the next thing you know the two of you are singing gospel together!

Aubrey

When I first met Aubrey in the care home she was alone at the shuffleboard table. I greeted her warmly and suggested that we walk around the garden. Although she seemed a bit suspicious of me, she agreed to walk with me when I told her that her son had sent me to be her companion. We were soon chatting easily and she became more trusting.

It was apparent that Aubrey's memory was failing. However, she was easy to talk to. Right off the bat, she mentioned that she was keen on the game of bridge. She was eager to pair up if I was interested. Unfortunately, I have never played bridge and I doubted that anyone in the care facility would be capable of playing with her.

We did try to play bingo that afternoon, though, in the facility organized bingo game. I showed her where to put the bingo dots and, even though we never won anything, we zealously "high-fived" each other! Although sometimes her words got muddled and her thoughts strayed, she had an excellent wit. I could tell early on that we were going to get along well together.

Week after week, she eagerly joined me for drives along the shoreline, chats at the beach and hot beverages that we purchased at local coffee shops. Aubrey really enjoyed the sea air and the bright sun. Even if it was cloudy, she was happy to get out of the vehicle and walk. Inclement weather did not faze her because she had been an avid all-season golfer. Getting out of the care home was a welcome change for her, rain or shine.

I had to be careful, though, because she was a bit unsteady on her feet a lot of the time. Her son and I attributed that to the variety of medications that her doctor had prescribed for her. The nurses would dole out her anti-anxiety medication so that she would not pace, or go in and out of the other resident's rooms. She would lose her eyeglasses and her television remote on a daily basis. She would also take other people's possessions from their rooms.

When we were out together, she was so appreciative. She thanked me many times in between deep breaths of fresh air and sighs of pleasure. Although she did have her down days, being with her was a delight. A couple of times she asked me what she had done to be put in "jail" and what, if anything, could be done to get her "released." I told her that she had done nothing wrong and that her family had put her in a care home for her own protection. They traveled a lot and did not want her to get lost or injured. I told her that the safest place for her was at the care home where she was living.

In spite of her confusion, though, she did have some happy times while she was in my company. Let me share with you some of my most poignant memories. One memory is of an event that occurred very shortly after our first meeting. As we passed a baseball field, she commented, "If I died watching one of my grandchildren playing sports, I would die happy." Her idea of

Aubrey

Heaven on Earth was attending a sporting event. Although it may have seemed like an appealing place to cross over, I am sure it would have been a huge shock for her grandkids, had it actually happened during one of their games!

The other solid gold moment occurred just days before Thanksgiving. I had handed her a piece of paper and a crayon, and we doodled a bit. I drew some leaves and bright orange flowers, and then I asked, "What are you thankful for?" She said, "I am thankful for my family and for your friendship, and I am thankful for the opportunity to learn." Yes, she had dementia. But, at times, she seemed to be fully present and knew what she was saying. That meant a lot to both of us.

Often, after we had been out together, I would leave her in her room, dozing in the easy chair with the television tuned to the sports channel. She found it comforting to hear the familiar sounds of a crowd roaring, a referee whistling or an umpire shouting. When the staff came in to take her for her lunch, they would find her either napping or staring blissfully at a game that was in progress.

Unfortunately, Aubrey's ability to leave the care home diminished. One of the last times I took her out was on a November day. The air was crisp and, since I was taking her to her granddaughter's wedding at a seaside hotel, I dressed her in appropriate and warm clothes for the occasion. She wore a pair of stylish pants and a colorful sweater beneath a stylish hat and a grey winter coat.

Aubrey

As we arrived at the charming little hotel all of her grandchildren stood to greet her. The ceremony took place on a patio that overlooked the Pacific Ocean and, even though she was dressed warmly and wore a pair of black leather gloves on her hands, I still placed a blanket over her lap and seated us close to the outdoor patio heater.

No doubt some family members who had not seen her for a while were shocked by how she had aged and by how thin she had become. She smiled at all of them and seemed genuinely pleased to be there. That was short lived because, even with all of my precautionary efforts, it was not long before she looked as if she was chilled to the bone. Near the end of the ceremony I took her inside. We watched it through the glass and clapped when the couple finished saying their vows. After that, she said to me, "Please can we go now? Please!" We did not stay for refreshments. Instead, I honored her request and asked two of her good-looking grandsons to walk her to my car.

On the drive back to town we stopped at a fast food, drive-through restaurant, and picked up a burger and a coffee. A short time later we had to make a toileting stop. While I was giving her some assistance I was taken aback by how bony she had become. I realized that I had truly taken a huge risk by bringing her out that day. If she had fallen while she was in my care, I would have felt terrible. Certainly some serious harm could have come to her. The family had trusted me, though. They were appreciative that I could help them celebrate on their special day. It would have been very difficult for them to manage the logistics of getting Aubrey from the care home and of transporting her an hour's journey. A day or two later, a Thank You card arrived in my mailbox. It contained some cash, as an expression of their gratitude for making sure that the matriarch was in attendance.

About six months later, Aubrey suffered a fall, during which she broke her hip. I visited her in the hospital after the "repair job" and, although she was delirious from the surgery, she smiled and said to me, "They sure make good coffee in here." I told her son what she had said to me. He laughed and assured me that she had not been allowed to consume any liquids after her operation. She must have dreamed about the coffee.

Aubrey started the latter part of her life by getting about in a wheelchair. She adapted to it quite well. She really took another one of life's setbacks with great dignity. Every Friday, I would wheel her out on the veranda, take her down to the library and sit with her during lunch. Her eyes always lit up when she saw me. She always thanked me for coming to see her. One day, out of the blue, she said to me very coherently, "If only there were more people like you."

Shortly before Christmas, I went to see her. I was about to take a vacation. She was bedridden and barely conscious. I said, "Aubrey, it's me." She smiled a faint smile. I put some water on a spoon and put it gently to her lips. She managed to take a small sip. "Good-bye. I am going away for a while. You are loved. Your family loves you. I love you. See you in the New Year." Again she gave me a faint smile.

Just before dawn on New Year's Day, I dreamed about a small bird sitting in the bottom of a cage. It had the head and beak of a swallow. It was almost lifeless as it lifted its little head slightly to look at me. I gave it some water from a dropper. It took a few drops, and then seemed to perk up a little. Then it put its head back down. When I awoke, I said to my husband, "I think Aubrey may have passed away. I just had one of my significant bird dreams."

Sure enough, when I returned a week or so later, her son emailed me and gave me the news. He said, "Mom passed away in the early hours of January 2nd." After not eating or drinking for over a week, she went peacefully. I guess that, at the time I dreamed about the swallow, Aubrey was drifting in and out of this world. Perhaps the soul flutters around the body, much like a bird, and then it wings its way to the afterlife at the time of death.

Her son went on to say, "We are so thankful for the friendship you had with her. While you never saw the full capacity Aubrey, I know you experienced her essence - that spark of energy and sense of humor that defined her."

A few days later, I attended a memorial that was held for her. As I walked into the small chapel, I was aware of the music that was playing through the speakers. It was not typical of most church music. It was lively and jazzy. I recognized it as *"Ain't Misbehavin,"* a Rod Stewart remake of the old Louis Armstrong hit. I felt like I should be dancing. I bet Aubrey was. I focused on the urn that held her ashes. It was a beautiful purple and blue color. However, what really caught my eye were the swallows that were painted on it! I grinned ear to ear. I have an infatuation with swallows. Every year I wait for the violet-green tree swallows to return to their nests in my yard. There was even more of a significance now, however, as I recalled my dream about the swallow in the cage.

At the request of Aubrey's son, I stood up and read from the Gospel according to Matthew:

Blessed are the poor in spirit, for theirs is the kingdom of heaven.

Blessed are those who mourn for they will be comforted.

Blessed are the meek, for they will inherit the earth.

Blessed are those who hunger and thirst for righteousness, for they will be filled.

"Rejoice and be glad, for your reward is great in heaven"

As I walked out of the service, I knew that Aubrey was rejoicing. The music of *"Ol' Blue Eyes"* playing out of the speakers confirmed it. *"Heaven, I'm in heaven..."*

Tip:

Spend a few minutes expressing gratitude. You can take turns talking about "thankfulness," and then draw what it looks like.

Bea

It was hard to find a card that had the right sentiment for the family of a lady who lived to be 105 years of age! Typical sympathy cards just didn't seem appropriate for this time of loss. Bea wasn't just any lady; she was my dear friend. She had such a positive outlook on life and also on death. She lived life as though each day was a blessing.

I met Bea when she was in her late nineties. We met through a mutual friend, named Louise, at Louise's ninetieth birthday party. Bea encouraged me to bring her over for tea whenever I could manage it.

In spite of poor eyesight and poor hearing, darling Bea had a mind that was as sharp as a tack. She was often the co-coordinator of memorial gatherings, and of small luncheons and tea parties for two. Bea didn't do all of this hosting single-handedly, though. She had help from two wonderful daughters, and grandchildren galore. It was because of family members who adored her that she was able to live in her own modest home, that is, until mobility issues restricted her from remaining there.

When her house was sold to a nice young family, Bea moved into a nursing home. It was actually a transitional place that was temporary until a more suitable permanent lodging could be secured. It was here that I visited her, in a nice bright room that overlooked a garden.

Bea

I asked Bea about her state of being. She replied, "I vowed that I would be happy, no matter where they put me." Her smile was genuine. She continued, "...and I am happy."

Not long after that, she had to be moved to another facility. Her new room was on one of the higher floors of the building where garden access was not particularly easy. However, when she could get someone to push her wheelchair for her, she would go outside to breathe the fresh air. Usually, her daughters would visit on alternate days, so Bea felt anything but lonely. She had decided to be happy here also.

Although Bea's handwriting became shaky, it didn't stop her from sending me a Christmas card every year. I delighted in showing people the cards I had received from my centenarian gal-pal. Whenever I would buy a greeting card for Bea's birthday, I found it fun to ask the clerk if they had anything that congratulated someone who was over one hundred years old! After finding something suitable I signed my name and wrote "WOW!" on her card.

Whenever I called her, her strong voice would greet me on the other end of the telephone line. Her keen mind retained bits of information that I had previously relayed to her, so she would inquire about my children and what they were involved in.

One November day, I received a call from one of her daughters informing me that her mother had passed away peacefully. She had been "with it" right up until about a week prior to leaving this world. I didn't cry when I heard the news. I smiled broadly because I had known such a remarkable woman.

On the day of Bea's funeral I awakened with *"Beethoven's 9th Symphony"* playing in my head. The words to *"Ode to Joy"* sprang from my lips.

Joyful, joyful we adore Thee,

God of glory, Lord of love;

hearts unfold like flowers before Thee,

opening to the sun above.

Melt the clouds of sin and sadness,

drive the dark of doubt away;

giver of immortal gladness,

fill us with the light of day.

When I walked into the small chapel, I picked up the program. It read, "Thanksgiving for the life of Bea." To my delight, I found the words to *"Ode To Joy"* printed on the back of the folded document. It was the only song that had been chosen for us to sing at her parting celebration! I have nothing but assurance that Bea is now joyfully sitting in the garden of eternal happiness. Way to go, Bea. WOW!

Tip:

When on holidays be sure and send postcards. Encourage grandchildren to send postcards too. If possible write in black ink and large print. Or, write a note for care home staff to read the postcard aloud to your loved one.

Dad

Darling daughter," said my father, "I hope you'll have time to spend with *me* when I get dementia."

"You bet I will, Dad," was my response. He emphasized the word "me" because he knew how much time I spent being a companion to others who had dementia.

Dementia runs in our family. My grandfather, my great uncle and my great grandmother all suffered from some form of senility. My grandfather, that is, my Dad's father, was diagnosed with Alzheimer's disease when I was in my teens.

It started gradually for my father. There were times when he would stare off into space. He'd look a little dazed when he and my mother and I were out shopping. "Keep an eye on your father," Mom would caution. "He might not know where we are."

He was good about using his cellphone though. In fact, the grandchildren taught him how to text messages and he would text all of us many times a day, and also at night. Some of the most humorous messages came at 3:00 am. Although he was having trouble sleeping, I wasn't. So I learned to turn off my cellphone at night so that I wouldn't receive his messages until the morning.

It's 3:00 am and I have just been for a walk outside. The moon is magnificent. Have you seen it? and *Don't tell your mother I was out. She who must be obeyed would not be pleased.*

Dad

While I checked my morning emails, I would see that he had also been busy on his computer sending me more information about his cellphone! Apparently, he thought it had died and needed a new battery. He sent me this update:

Well, I cheerfully proclaim my cellphone to be healthy, wealthy and wise. What happened, you may ask? (and I shall modestly, answer). I tapped it substantially, on the back-side: from whence appeareth (from the frontal side) a well-lit, bright and jolly smile. "All is well," it proclaimeth...

I am very fortunate to have saved dozens of emails, cards, letters, drawings and humorous cartoons from my father. I would often receive letters from him in the mail, even though we lived in the same city. Here's an excerpt from one. It had a gift of money enclosed:

In thinking about your work with the elderly I can't help but admire what you have been doing these past years, what emotional experiences, mostly upon the passing of those souls whom you have helped, and the realization that you will not be able to continue this kind of work forever....just too draining upon your precious self!

...this cheque is for your December birthday, which I can't wait to celebrate!

When his mind became so boggled that he could no longer live safely at home with my mother, I was there for him. I felt awful that I couldn't look after him full-time, but he needed to be

Dad

in a care facility where the doors were safely locked around the clock.

For the most part, Dad was content, but he was unfamiliar with the routine of such an institution. It wasn't really "home," but we did our best to make it feel that way. There were photos on his bulletin board and picture albums on his desk. We decorated his walls with a few things from home.

I visited him at least twice a week. My mother visited him nearly every day. The grandchildren stopped by for a chat, and a hug or two. I even hired a paid companion for him.

It seemed strange to me that I, a paid companion to others, would hire a paid companion for my own father. Over time, it began to feel comfortable because Gloria was exactly the right person for the job. She was a family friend who had a personal connection with Dad and, gave my mom and I a break by spending Sunday afternoon reading with him and taking him for walks.

He wasn't always sure about Gloria though. I would say, "Gloria will be here later today to see you." When he'd ask, "Do I know her?" I would show him the photo of her that was pinned to his bulletin board. "Oh yes, that will be wonderful," he would say in a now-reassured voice.

Gloria always brought a doughnut for Dad, and a cup of hot chocolate or decaf coffee. They had a nice time together. He'd always thank her for coming to see him. Her visits with my father were usually quite subdued, but very meaningful. Mine were a little more animated.

Dad

"Halleluiah!" Dad would proclaim loudly when I would come through his door.

"Thank goodness you're here! I was just thinking about you!"

"Do you want to go for a ride, Dad?"

"YOU BET I DO!" was almost always his response.

Since Dad had been a floatplane pilot, we'd go watch the planes that were taking off and landing. We'd sit by the water and he'd sip his milkshake contentedly through a straw. "Mmmmmm, this sure is good."

"Glad you're enjoying it." While I said this, I would usually lean into him or lovingly pat his hand.

On the way back to the care home, he often complimented me on my driving skills. I would respond, "I learned from the best teachers, Dad." Then pausing, I would add, "You and Mom!" He'd smile ear-to-ear.

The geriatric psychiatrist had prescribed some anti-anxiety medications for Dad. His frontal lobe, which is the part of the brain that controls emotion, logic and reason, had been damaged by small strokes, called T.I.A.s. The pills were supposed to control his nervousness. The down side was that the medication slowed him down and made him sleep more.

When he first went into a care facility, Dad could walk on his own. After he was medicated, he started using a walker. It wasn't long before he needed a wheelchair for longer trips. During his final days he declined rapidly and needed a mechanical hoist

Dad

just to get out of bed. He went from being able to hold a bit of a conversation to barely being able to speak at all. In just one week, he could no longer feed himself.

He still recognized Mom and I, and most of his family, though. He could still say, "I love you." Faint words of prayers could be heard from his lips. He had committed important and sacred quotes to memory. Dad, being a devoted member of the Bahá'í Faith, could still recite many meaningful passages from the writings.

Our entire family played a part in Dad's passing. My brothers, and their spouses and children arrived to be with him in person. Some relatives telephoned and we put the phone to his ear so that he could hear them speak.

Those who were in attendance at his bedside spent the entire day singing and speaking to him, even into the evening. Since hearing is the last of the five senses to go, Dad heard many of his favorite jazz melodies, sacred verses, and old wartime songs. Some of us took turns wiping my father's fevered brow. Others brought tea and sweets. We'd sit outside in the garden and reminisce about the good times with "Gramps."

Then it was all over - a life so sweet. When we all slipped out of the room for a moment, he exhaled for the final time. My mother was the first to receive the news. "He's gone," the nurse said when Mom walked back into his room. I received the news next. I had just gone out to the parking lot to make a bed for myself in the car when my cellphone rang.

Dad

My brothers and I and their families cried, but it wasn't long before we rejoiced together and said prayers for Dad's soul to wing its way to the next world.

Mom, also a Bahá'í, took solace from these sacred words:

"I have made death a messenger of joy to thee. Wherefore dost thou grieve?"

After 61 years of marriage, she had lost her partner from this realm of existence, but she really didn't feel sorrowful. She said that she had grieved his passing before he passed away. She saw him slipping away from her with his diminishing mental faculties. That was more painful to her than his death itself.

When I was preparing for dear Dad's funeral, I scrolled through my emails and found the ones that we had exchanged over the years. One in particular caught my eye. It was written the day before Dad was admitted to the hospital a year and a half earlier.

"Darling daughter, I shall love you for all eternity."

I felt that this was his answer to a prayer I had whispered so many times.

"Let my heart be dilated with joy through the spirit of confirmation from Thy kingdom..." *

I have made death a messenger of joy to thee.
Wherefore dost thou grieve?
~ Bahá'u'lláh

sacred writings of the Bahá'í Faith

Useful Tips:

Keep lip balm with resident's name on it to apply to their parched lips. Since many of the care homes and hospitals have stale, dry air. This will be very soothing.

Encourage residents to drink more water

Set up a digital photo display and regularly add new pictures to it. Seeing pictures scrolling past is comforting for someone whose family may live far away.

Bring magazines and newspapers to show and flip through together.

Read the horoscopes for fun

Try to do a crossword puzzle together. You read the clues and see if they can come up with the answers.

Book a wheelchair equipped taxi and go sight seeing.

For more tips, ideas, quotes, addresses, and dialogue please go to my website: www.makingdyingjoyful.com

Made in the USA
Charleston, SC
19 November 2013